Legacy of Stone

SASKATCHEWAN'S STONE BUILDINGS

Margaret Hryniuk & Frank Korvemaker

PHOTOGRAPHS BY Larry Easton

Margaret Hryniuk

COTEAU BOOKS

Edited by Bobbi Coulter.
Book and cover design by Duncan Campbell.

Printed and bound in Canada at Friesens.

LIBRARY AND ARCHIVES CANADA CATALOGUING IN PUBLICATION

Hryniuk, Margaret, 1939-
     Legacy of stone : Saskatchewan's stone buildings / Margaret
Hryniuk, Frank Korvemaker ; photographs by Larry Easton.

ISBN 978-1-55050-369-2

     1. Stone buildings—Saskatchewan—History. 2. Stone
buildings—Saskatchewan—Pictorial works. 3. Architects and
builders—Saskatchewan—Biography. 4. Architecture—Saskatchewan—
History—Pictorial works. I. Korvemaker, Frank II. Easton, Larry, 1938-
III. Title.

NA746.S3H79 2008   721'.0441097124   C2008-905722-8

2517 Victoria Ave.
Regina, Saskatchewan
Canada   S4P 0T2

AVAILABLE IN CANADA & THE US FROM
Fitzhenry & Whiteside
195 Allstate Parkway
Markham, Ontario, Canada, L3R 4T8

The publisher gratefully acknowledges the financial assistance of the Saskatchewan Arts
Board, the Canada Council for the Arts, the Government of Canada through the Book
Publishing Industry Development Program (BPIDP), Association for the Export of Canadian
Books, the Saskatchewan Heritage Foundation, and the City of Regina Arts Commission,
for its publishing program.

10 9 8 7 6 5 4 3 2 1

CONTENTS

House at Bird's Point, in the Qu'Appelle
Valley, photographed by Cecil
and Susan Howard.

to Cecil and Susan Hayward

Several people have attempted to catalogue late nineteenth- and early twentieth-century Saskatchewan stone buildings, but the most comprehensive study undertaken to date was the "Inventory of Stone Buildings in Saskatchewan" conducted by the late Cecil Hayward and his wife Susan of Assiniboia. They started their research and photography in the early 1980s, and have devoted the past twenty-five years to this one-time hobby. An example of their photography is illustrated by this attractive house at Bird's Point, in the Qu'Appelle Valley. ❧ This project became for them a labour of love. They searched through local history books, contacted local administrators, talked with owners of stone buildings, published requests in weekly papers, and ferreted out information from some unusual sources. Their work is the foundation upon which any future stone buildings projects will be built. In recognition of their unique contribution, we dedicate this book to them. Although Cec passed before this book was published, we expect that he would have enjoyed reading it as much as he and Susan did travelling across the province to find and record the remaining stone buildings. ❧

OPPOSITE: The last vestige of a stone building near Limerick disintegrates with each passing year.

Why Stone?

FOREWORD

When the Hudson's Bay Company decided in 1896 to build a store in Fort Qu'Appelle, they no doubt wanted a design that was up-to-date, attractive, and inviting; one that would be solid and require little maintenance. The resulting building incorporated a front façade of brick. From the buff colour, we can speculate that the brick came from the Pelletier brickyard just a few kilometres to the east, on Katepwa Lake, or from one of the many brick plants situated along the main line of the Canadian Pacific Railway between Winnipeg and Regina in the late nineteenth century. The sides and back of the store were constructed from stone, likely gathered in the coulees and slopes of the Qu'Appelle Valley. Brick, a manufactured material, was clearly more highly valued than the utilitarian fieldstone.

The Roy Rivers medicine wheel, on the Missouri Coteau. (George Toth)

boulders of the Hudson's Bay Store in Fort Qu'Appelle, the beauty of fieldstone is undisputed. It is a material from *this* place and *this* landscape. It looks good in any of our four distinct seasons and in the clear sunlight that is one of the defining aspects of Saskatchewan.

Stone is a thread that extends through all of the various styles and time periods of architecture and building in Saskatchewan. It extends all the way back to the enigmatic constructions of the First Nations, the stone teepee rings, medicine wheels, and figures that dotted the landscape. It appears on the modernist buildings of the 1950s, 1960s and 1970s, adding a humanizing influence to a style often criticized for being cold and austere. It still appears on buildings today, especially when durability and image are important.

Stone is relevant for contemporary buildings. We no longer think of heading out to the fields to gather building materials before starting a construction project. We have so many manufactured materials available that we have

Just a dozen years later, when the Board of Governors for the University of Saskatchewan decided in 1908 that the university should be built in the Collegiate Gothic style and the building material would be stone, the architects, Brown and Vallance of Montreal, specified rough-cut Tyndall stone for the exterior of one of the first structures, the College Building. The discovery of a supply of fieldstone north of the campus resulted in the first budget cut for a U of S construction project, and the tradition of using local fieldstone on the campus was begun.

Why stone? One simple reason is that stone is beautiful. Whether it is the dolomite limestone called greystone at the University of Saskatchewan or the granite

lost the idea of representing a particular place through its materials. With an increasing concern for environmental issues, however, stone as a building material is again relevant, and the idea of "gathering" materials through deconstruction and re-use, and allowing the design to be driven by the materials rather than the other way around, is gaining ground. This book shows that stone has a future by illustrating wonderful examples from the past that convey the beauty and durability of one of the oldest building materials. 🌿

Bernard Flaman, SAA, MRAIC
Heritage Architect, Public Works and Government Services Canada

ABOVE: The 1966 College of Law building at the University of Saskatchewan. (Henry Kalen)

LEFT: Stonemasons, bricklayers, and carpenters build the Hudson's Bay Company (HBC) store at Fort Qu'Appelle in 1897. (Saskatchewan Archives Board R-B 9979)

Introduction

"If only these old walls could talk, what a story they would tell." Wherever buildings and structures have survived from one generation to another, from one millennium to another, we find ourselves asking: "Who made this?" and "What happened here?" Because stone is beautiful but also durable and therefore permanent, people use it to build structures that they think are important, and hence they remain so to us. Whether it is a public building like a school or a church or a private home, the use of stone signals to us that our forebears cared deeply enough about a place that they invested their money, time and effort – the sweat of their brow – in erecting something of permanence and beauty.

But it is not just the structure that is interesting; it is also the people who lived within it.

The photographs and stories in this book will give you more than an understanding of why Saskatchewan people built with stone, who some of those builders were, and what this particular construction material meant to them. You may get a sense that these old stone walls are transmitting some of their stories to you, stories of the life and times of their people.

Saskatchewan's stone buildings display a wide variety of stones, from the rugged natural fieldstones commonly seen in many prairie farmyards to the finely tooled and highly polished cut stones on many commercial and public buildings. Although the total number of stone buildings constructed in Saskatchewan many never be known, a review of existing inventories, local history books, and historical photographs in various archives suggests that it is probably between five hundred and one thousand. Although these figures may seem small to some, it is actually quite remarkable that this many stone buildings were built here, considering the scarcity of stone in the southern half of the province, where the vast majority of people settled.

While Saskatchewan's best-known and most elaborate quarried stone building is the Legislative Building in Regina, this book deals primarily with fieldstone buildings, those built of stones gathered from fields around the province. Buildings made with fieldstones reflect the craftsmanship of local stonemasons, whether the stones appear to be randomly laid or split and squared and placed in neat rows or almost symmetrical patterns. We have selected approximately fifty fieldstone buildings in Saskatchewan to illustrate the enduring beauty of this type of building material. Most were constructed late in the nineteenth and early twentieth centuries during a period of extensive immigration and settlement in Canada. We chose them based on a combination of features, including attractiveness, minimal alteration, and historic interest and significance.

While a substantial number of stone residences, farm buildings, and churches have survived into the twenty-first century, many of the schools from that era have disappeared. Similarly, most stone commercial buildings have been either demolished or so radically renovated that little of the original fine workmanship of the stonemason is evident today. Hence, commercial buildings have not been included in this publication, except in the Historical Overview. Nor are the finely crafted Tyndall stone buildings found in government and other institutional complexes. They are subjects for another book.

As you read through the following chapters, you too will see why stone is such an evocative building material, and why stone has been the construction material of choice throughout the world. Indeed, the stones illustrated in this book do talk, and speak of the natural forces that created them, and of the workmen who selected their finest features and incorporated them into some of Saskatchewan's most interesting historic buildings.

This book first takes a brief look at the early use of stone in our province, and then at some of the stonemasons – the people who built these magnificent structures. Then we examine farmhouses, the earliest stone buildings to be erected in the province, and we feature some of the more interesting structures, such as the Bell farmhouse and round barn, which were built in 1882 as the crews building the Canadian Pacific Railway passed through the Indian Head district. Stone houses were also built in the new towns springing up along the CPR mainline. We highlight several stone schools, a fair number of which were built, but very few which stand today. Churches have a much better survival rate, and many fine pioneer stone churches still grace the province. We end the book with a look at some of the few public buildings that were made of fieldstone.

All photographs are the work of Larry and Dorothy Easton unless otherwise noted. Specific images taken by Dorothy are listed in the Acknowledgements. ❦

Historical Overview

Fieldstones have always been an integral part of Aboriginal people's relationship to the environment. Stones were the essence of human and animal effigies and ceremonial circles, creating tangible places sacred to the people. Stones were also used to create drive-lines for herding bison to cliff edges, to make tools and decorative items, and for aspects of their dwellings. However, rather than constructing buildings, as was the case in more southern North American Aboriginal cultures, the original prairie inhabitants used fieldstones to hold down the coverings of their portable dwellings, commonly called teepees. These stones were readily available across the land, part of the debris left on the prairie when

An Indian encampment at the Qu'Appelle Valley. (Archives of Ontario S 12771)

a glacier covering much of the prairie retreated northeastward about 12,000 years ago.

As these people moved from one location to another, the remnants of their villages and campsites were marked by stone circles – now called teepee rings. While many of these traces of their presence on the prairie have vanished, a significant number of teepee rings and other stone features are still visible in areas that were never cultivated, and remind us of a time when the entire prairie was populated by these people.

Starting in the 1730s, during the French Regime in Canada, explorers and fur traders from Quebec began to erect trading posts in the West. They were followed in the 1770s by their English counterparts based out of Hudson Bay. Over the next century, an extensive commercial fur-trading network stretched across the northern portion of the North American continent. The Hudson's Bay Company and the North West Company, the two best-known corporations, built trading posts along the major waterways, which provided the best access to the rich fur-bearing regions of the country.

While their trading posts

One of the old stone chimneys at Cumberland House, 1923. (Library and Archives Canada: PAC 19258)

were generally made of logs, they often made fireplaces and chimneys of stone, and traces of these can now be seen at a small number of historic sites around the province. Occasionally, special buildings such as powder magazines, used to store gun powder, were also made of stone to prevent serious damage in case of explosions. The 1886 powder magazine at the Hudson's Bay Company's post at Cumberland House stands as the lone Saskatchewan example of this kind of fieldstone structure.

In 1870 the government of Canada acquired jurisdiction over the Canadian interior from the Hudson's Bay Company and began a number of initiatives to settle these lands. The Dominion Lands (Homestead) Act of 1872 initiated a process of railway construction and gradual population increase on the Canadian prairie. In 1896, the newly elected Laurier government focused great attention and effort into rapid settlement of the western interior by settlers from other countries. Between 1870 and 1930, in the space of just over half a century, the face of western Canada was dramatically changed, primarily due to the development of roads, railways, towns and, most noticeably, the chequered pattern of land surveying arbitrarily imposed across most of the prairie.

This massive influx of people, accustomed to living and working in buildings made of varying styles and architectural designs, provided great opportunities for those involved in the construction industry. Among them were stonemasons, some trained in their country of origin, others acquiring knowledge of the trade while in Canada. While much of their work involved building foundations for frame structures, many were also employed in the construction of complete stone houses, schools, churches, stores and barns.

Wherever possible, construction took advantage of the natural environment. Hence, in the north, where trees grew in abundance, many buildings were made first of logs, then of wood frame, as sawmills began to provide the necessary lumber. On the open prairie, where lumber was at best scarce and often totally impossible to find, many settlers resorted to building their first homes and barns out of sod cut from the natural prairie, or to importing lumber from other regions of the continent. Others gathered stones from the shores of creeks and rivers or along glacial deposits and hired stonemasons to erect foundations or complete stone buildings for them.

Fieldstones were generally used in their natural state, or split and formed into squares and rectangles. Generally the stones used were those that were readily accessible to the building project. However, some masons favoured granite for its colour variations, or dolomite limestone because it could be readily split. Quarried stones had to be brought in from places such as Stonewall and Tyndall, Manitoba, and tended to be used only for more important structures.

Stone construction not only took advantage of one of the few natural building materials on the prairie, it was fireproof. However, wood frame buildings were easier and quicker to erect, and often lumber, while not readily available, could be brought to the community by train. It was certainly cheaper to import lumber than it was to bring in stone or brick. Hence, many prairie towns at the turn of the twentieth century were largely composed of wooden buildings, and when a fire occurred, major sections of the town were destroyed as a result of one small initial blaze. Consequently, some communities passed bylaws

ABOVE: John and Harry Howard moving field-stones in the Whitewood area, 1910 – never an easy task. (Saskatchewan Archives Board R-A 6190)

RIGHT: Commercial buildings in Moose Jaw in 1898, showing transition from wooden to masonry buildings, along with a pile of stones ready for further construction. (Moose Jaw Public Library/Archives 73–169)

requiring merchants to construct replacement buildings out of masonry – either brick or stone – to help retard the spread of future fires. Moose Jaw, for instance, after suffering the loss of eighteen structures, including a church, in a December 1891 fire, passed just such a bylaw for all new construction in the main downtown business area.

People chose stone not only for its resistance to fire, however, but also because it represented durability and prosperity. For major public institutions, such as schools and churches, the use of stone reflected the community's pride in its ability to build well, and indicated a sense of permanence. For the new frontier, masonry construction, whether of brick or stone, visibly displayed the success of the pioneers and their faith in the future growth of their communities. For some, stone spoke of their personal achievement as they replaced their initial homestead shack first with a frame structure, then with a larger brick or stone building. Others came from a tradition of building with stone, and expressed some tangible remembrance of their ancestral heritage by residing in a stone house designed to reflect the architecture of their homeland.

Geographically, more stone buildings were erected in the southern portion of the province than elsewhere. This is partly due to the fact that the southeast opened for settlement earlier than much of the rest of Saskatchewan, at a time when alternate building materials were scarce. In addition, many of those settlers came from Ontario, where building with stone was a common practice. Indeed, some of the homes seen along the Trans-Canada Highway

region look strikingly similar to those found in Peterborough and Lindsay.

The use of stone declined as other less expensive or more practical building materials became available. The influx of lumber from both the east and west on newly constructed railway lines brought this inexpensive material into ready access throughout the prairies. In addition, as clays suitable for making bricks began to be discovered and exploited, many small brick factories were established, thus providing an easy-to-use and readily available masonry product. Stones were still popular, but were not as convenient and often more expensive to use. And, while stone buildings tended to be made of solid walls up to a metre thick, brick buildings could be thinner, and often were composed of a relatively thin veneer over a frame wall structure.

Nevertheless, stone remains a popular building material. At the turn of the twenty-first century, however, few new buildings are made with fieldstone, the preferred material being machine-cut stones, some with a rugged surface. This too has been cut into a thin veneer, and, like brick, is applied over a wood frame wall. In addition, synthetic stone has become increasingly popular, reflecting the eternal allure of this exceptional building material. ❧

Public School, Estevan: Originally erected in 1894, substantially enlarged in 1904, and demolished in 1955. (Saskatchewan Archives Board R-B 804–1)

King's Hotel, Balgonie, shortly after completion; now demolished. (Saskatchewan Archives Board R-A 22,320)

The Stonemasons

The life of a stonemason was difficult. The stones were heavy, and the makeshift wooden scaffolding dangerous. Nevertheless, it also presented certain rewards that few other trades could match: a completed product which would potentially last many years beyond the life of its creator. As well, the wages for stonemasons were considered desirable – approximately double those of a carpenter, and triple those of the common labourer. The higher wages for bricklayers and stonemasons reflect the importance the industry placed on these tradesmen. ❧ Stonemasonry is one of the oldest trades in the world, and along with that of the carpenter, it was one of the earlier trades to be recorded in present-day Saskatchewan. The work of the stonemason was first applied during the late eighteenth century, when

foundations, fireplaces and chimneys were constructed for the various fur trade posts. The art of laying stone was a serious business, and critical to the efficient operation of a fireplace and chimney. Some of the stonework was "dry masonry" – without the use of mortar – which required even greater talent.

Most stonemasons, however, preferred to incorporate mortar to provide extra strength for the structure and to help keep the elements out. In many instances, the stonemasons themselves made their own lime for mortar by quarrying limestone and then burning it in a lime kiln until it broke down. Vertical holes were sometimes drilled into the stone in the fall, filled with water, and capped; the resultant expansion due to freeze-thaw cycles helped break up the stone for easier quarrying and working the following spring or summer.

The stonemason's work blossomed in the late nineteenth and early twentieth centuries, as settlers began to populate the prairie and parkland areas of the province. While some stonemasons came as settlers, many soon realized that there was a significant demand for their trade in the construction of farmhouses, barns, schools, churches and commercial buildings. Stone was not as readily available as in many parts of eastern Canada, but many settlers were only too glad to be rid of what they saw as an impediment to their farming operations, and in numerous instances stonepickers could harvest them freely.

Many stonemasons originated in the British Isles; others came from eastern Canada, the United States and various European countries. Like most of the other construction trades at the time, the stonemason trade was dominated by men.

Well over two hundred stonemasons constructed buildings in Saskatchewan before the middle of the twentieth century, including Adam

Motherwell homestead, near Abernethy, one of Cantelon's best-known structures.

Cantelon, Moffat and Abernethy; Karl Gortzyk, Frenchman Butte; J. Hutson, Moffat; the Kent family, Saskatoon; William McCall, Moffat; Robert McIlvenna and William McIlvenna, Oxbow; Nels H. Neilson, Yorkton; Charlie Parker and Harold Parker, Cardross and Wawota; Peter Reiger, Lemberg; George Rooks, Estevan; and Richard Talmay, Wapella.

Only two Saskatchewan women, Anna Klein of Francis and Mrs. Kanta of Valor, have been identified as being possible stonemasons. The lives of four of the most important of these stonemasons are highlighted here.

ADAM CANTELON

Born in Ontario in 1857, Adam Cantelon moved west in 1883 with his brother David, settling on homesteads in the Duff area, southwest of Melville. By 1886 he was helping construct stone buildings in the region, and served as the postmaster of Lorlie from 1887 to 1897.

Over the course of his masonry career, he worked north and south of the Qu'Appelle Valley, including St. Andrew's Presbyterian (United) Church at Moffat in 1891 and the Little Stone Church west of Abernethy in 1892. He is best known for the construction of Lanark Place, the farm home of W. R. Motherwell, federal Minister of Agriculture, south of Abernethy. While working there in 1897, Cantelon suffered a fall that hampered his later work abilities. Nevertheless, he continued in the stonemasonry business for another nine years.

Adam Cantelon moved to the southwestern part of the province in 1909, settling near Piapot. Here he focused on farming rather than building construction. He died in 1948 at the age of ninety-one.

NELS HOLER NEILSON

While many Saskatchewan stonemasons plied their trade as their primary source of income, some appear to have practised this profession on a more casual basis, likely to augment their regular farm income. One of the latter was Nels H. Neilson.

Family records indicate that Nels Neilson was born in Norway in 1856, and immigrated to Canada at the age of twenty-five. He initially settled at Stonewall, Manitoba, where he worked at one of the stone quarries. In 1883 he moved to the Orkney part of the York Colony and took up a homestead on the northeast quarter of section 16, township 26, range 4, west of the 2nd meridian. Here Nels met Elizabeth Seatter, who had emigrated from the Isle of Westray, Orkney, Scotland; they were married in Stonewall on April 18, 1884. The couple had three children: George, Gertrude, and Mary, who died at the age of nine.

Neilson had apparently learned the stonemason's trade while working in Manitoba, and he periodically applied this knowledge for the good of the community. In 1893 he erected the Orkney Presbyterian Church, and four years later, the Orkney School, directly across the road. In addition, he built at least one private residence: a two-storey farmhouse, erected in 1897, about five kilometres north of Sheho.

Like many pioneers of his time, Nels's commitment to the community was extensive. He served as a justice of the peace and a director of the Yorkton Agricultural Society (1887). He was also a member of several fraternal organizations, including the Independent Order of Foresters Lodge #1918, the Odd Fellows, and the Orange Lodge. Nels

Neilson became a Canadian citizen on December 17, 1891, and died on March 17, 1902, at the young age of forty-six. Elizabeth then moved with George and Gertrude to Kylemore, about one hundred kilometres northwest of Yorkton.

CHARLIE PARKER & HAROLD PARKER

Charlie Parker was born into his profession. His father, Lewis, built their stone residence in the Bobcaygeon area near Peterborough, Ontario. Then, while still in his teens, Charlie worked as an apprentice to a stonemason relative in New York. He then practised his trade in Ontario and,

in 1905, married Rebecca Dewdney. With their three children – Harold, Mabel, and Ruby – they moved west in 1912, first to Saskatoon, then the following year to the Cardross area south of Moose Jaw, where other members of his family were located. There he continued to ply his masonry trade, building houses, barns, public buildings, utility buildings and various other structures. In 1930 he relocated to the Moose Mountain area, where he was commissioned by the provincial government to construct the chalet at the newly created Moose Mountain Provincial Park on Kenosee Lake. This structure has become one of

Lynn Perry farmhouse, near Wawota.

FAR LEFT: The Orkney school and church at Orcadia, northwest of Yorkton.

southern Saskatchewan's best-known stone buildings. Charlie died at age eighty in 1955 in Wawota, having spent all his working life as a stonemason. He is buried behind St. Paul's Anglican Church, Langbank, a building he had constructed almost twenty years earlier.

Charlie's trade carried on with his son, Harold, who built several structures, including a cobblestone house and barn for one of his family members in the Wawota area before moving to Vancouver Island.

RICHARD TALMAY

Richard Talmay enjoyed incorporating decorative red- or buff-coloured brick quoins into his stone building designs. He based his business out of Wapella, and constructed many of the stone buildings in communities along the main line of the Canadian Pacific Railway east of Indian Head. Indeed, the Grenfell Museum includes an illustrated tribute to his craftsmanship in that community alone. A century later, a substantial number of his buildings still stand, a testament to the qual-

ity of both his design and workmanship.

Born in England in 1843, Richard married Caroline Horton in 1872. For a while they lived in Chile to help build the docks of Valparaiso, then moved to Winnipeg in 1883, to Moosomin in 1890, and finally to a homestead in the Prosperity District northeast of Wapella in 1891. They had four children: Herbert, Harry, Emma, and Dick. For at least a decade, Talmay simultaneously farmed and operated his masonry construction business. While the two older boys initially helped their father with both his business and farm work, eventually all three men focused on farming their own homesteads. Richard Talmay died in 1921 at age seventy-eight and was buried in the Wapella cemetery. His obituary in the *Regina Leader* stated that "he was well known in many western towns as a builder who was more concerned with giving good value than in making money, and his ideals of honor would not permit him to touch a building having any connection with the liquor trade." ❧

Farmhouses & Barns

Fieldstone farm buildings are a Saskatchewan secret. Sometimes glimpsed, perhaps even photographed, by a venturesome few who wander off paved roads, they speak of permanence and impermanence at the same time. The secret? A lost daughter replaced by a stranger, a love child whose descendant saved the family home, a national figure who not only covered his children in kisses but also his three-year affair, a barn built by the knighted son of the contractor for the Grand Trunk Pacific Railway, and a bootlegger whose genteel home belied his source of income. Fieldstone farm buildings – an exposé.

Saskatchewan has a rich agricultural heritage, which was for many decades the backbone of the provincial economy. Although farming is no longer as central to the development of the province as it once was, farms continue to dominate the landscape in the southern half of the province. Expansive fields encircle every urban community, and shelterbelts of trees and brush mark the home base of an operational farm, or remnants of a farm that once thrived there. As with other aspects of Saskatchewan society, farming is undergoing continual change in order to remain a viable part of the economy. That has often resulted in the amalgamation of farms, and the resultant abandonment of farm homes, barns, windmills, and grain elevators. ⁂ Although farming was undertaken at

The Anderson stone farmhouse south of Balcarres displays a high-pitched gable dormer in the centre of the roof, a pediment on the porch roof over the front door, and decorative brackets, spindles, and barge-boards on both the porch and gable. Double segmented arches extend over the windows.

several fur trade posts and missions, full-scale cultivation of the prairie did not start until after the federal government took over control of the land from the Hudson's Bay Company and negotiated treaties with various First Nations. Subsequently, the Canadian government passed the Dominion Lands Act in 1872. This legislation enabled people to acquire a quarter-section (160 acres) of land for a $10 registration fee. Upon

completing certain provisions to cultivate and reside on the land, they were granted free title to the property. This parcel of land became known as the home quarter, and the people who settled the land were referred to as home-steaders. These farmers could reserve another quarter-section of land, called a pre-emption, which they would similarly work after meeting their obligations on the home quarter, potentially doubling

the size of their farm.

Full-scale cultivation did not get underway until the railway was completed in the early 1880s. The next half century saw a massive influx of people and a whole new society into the Canadian interior. For decades, farming was the mainstay of the Saskatchewan economy, and that success was often reflect-ed in the evolution of farm buildings from log and sod shacks on the open prairie into well-landscaped farm-yards sporting various barns and a substantial farmhouse of wood, brick, or stone.

Stone was readily available to many farmers as they began to settle and develop their farmsteads at the turn of the twentieth century, and many took advantage of this free building material to construct foundations for their homes and barns, or to build struc-tures entirely of fieldstone. Stones were an impediment to farm machinery, and they were continually being cleared by hand or by machine. In many instances, these stones were dumped in stone piles at the corner of a field, where they would not interfere with the operation of farm equipment. In other instances, the stones were hauled to creeks to form a dam or a rock ford to permit easy crossing.

Stonemasons working in a region often found very co-operative farmers who only too gladly gave away their stones to anyone willing to haul them off their land. Some farmers saw the stones as a potential source of income, however, and negotiated their sale. Picking and hauling stone from fields to the site for a farmhouse or barn was never an easy task, particularly in the era when oxen, horses and mules pulled the heavy-laden wagons or stoneboats.

Saskatchewan's surviving historic stone buildings are largely located outside its villages, towns and cities. The reasons for this are often economic, but also sentimental. Farmers regularly operated at a low profit margin, leaving little excess money for renovating a stone farmhouse. Likewise, farmers tended to make do and repair their farm buildings, to extend their substantial initial investment. Even when they

were abandoned, it cost more than it was worth in both time and money to demolish these structures. As well, there was a sentimental appreciation of "the old homestead," and the simple fact that a stone ruin is often much more attractive than its frame counterpart.

Many of the stone farm homes recorded over the past century are impressive in their overall design, scale and craftsmanship. They easily compete with their urban counterparts as community landmarks. While a substantial number now stand abandoned, others are being rehabilitated and will grace the Saskatchewan landscape for many years to come.

Farmers regularly built expansive barns, structures that were often more impressive than the homes that they built for their families. The success and wealth of a farmer was often visibly displayed in the magnificence of his barns and other outbuildings. As with farmhouses, barns varied in design and construction material. The log or sod structure that provided a minimal shelter for the farm animals

TOP: The Beckton farmhouse – better known as Didsbury – was the showpiece of Cannington Manor at the end of the nineteenth century. As with many fine stone buildings throughout Saskatchewan, it has not survived into the twenty-first century. (Saskatchewan Archives Board R-A 23,054–1)

BOTTOM: The Price farmhouse near Moosomin was constructed in the late nineteenth century, and featured a mansard roof with a decorative shingle pattern. It stands in sharp contrast to the log buildings in the background, which probably date to the first years of settlement, while the house represents the Price family's success after a number of years on their homestead. (Saskatchewan Archives Board R-A 3309)

The L-shaped barn at the University of Saskatchewan features a split fieldstone foundation, gambrel roof, ten cupola air vents, and several dozen sloped and gabled dormer windows. A hoist system for lifting hay into the loft is visible at the top of the roof at both ends. The stone fence in the foreground serves as a corral for the livestock. Due to the barn's immense size, the stone foundation also includes buttresses, a feature seldom found in agricultural structures.

and their feed was replaced as soon as possible with a more substantial frame building, often constructed on a stone footing, or incorporating a stone main floor, with a frame superstructure. This loft housed the hay for the animals, and elaborate designs were employed to maximize the volume of straw and feed that could be stored there. Loading the loft became a technical challenge, and a variety of commercially produced metal rail systems were available.

Probably the most common barn design on the Canadian prairie was a rectangular or L-shaped barn with a gambrel roof. More complex and expensive to construct than the simple gable-roofed barn, it provided maximum open space for hay storage. By the time settlement came to the West in the late nineteenth century, building plans for barns were readily available from various lumber companies. Nevertheless, a number of skilled local carpenters were able to construct barns from memory. In many instances, the resultant structure, the combined work of a stonemason and carpenter, still stands as a testament to both of their talents

One of the most impressive barn forms, and a rare feature in Saskatchewan, was the round barn. Approximately twenty such structures are

The Bartel round barn west of Drake features a full main floor to house the livestock. The work of stonemason Lorne Thompson and carpenter John Andres, it was completed in 1927.

known to have been built in Saskatchewan between 1882 and 1940, but few survive. The round barn reportedly provided certain efficiencies in operation, but the style never became popular on the prairies.

Two landmark stone barns in Saskatchewan are the Bell Farm round barn, located north of Indian Head, and the University Barn at the University of Saskatchewan in Saskatoon. Neither structure is particularly representative of farming in Saskatchewan. The former was built in 1882 as part of a corporate farm called the Qu'Appelle Valley Farming Company. Badly deteriorated after facing the harsh prairie environment for 125 years, the Bell barn is the oldest-known masonry barn in Saskatchewan. The University Barn was an institutional facility designed by Montreal architects Brown and Vallance, and built by the provincial government as part of its post-secondary agricultural education program. It took over two years to construct and was completed in 1912. Almost a century later, it still stands in excellent repair. ❧

Lanark Place

THE MOTHERWELL FARM, NEAR ABERNETHY

William Richard Motherwell was the co-founder of the Territorial Grain Growers' Association in 1901, Saskatchewan's Minister of Agriculture from 1905 to 1918, and federal Minister of Agriculture from 1922 to 1930. It was primarily for these reasons that his farmstead near Abernethy was declared a national historic site, meticulously restored to its 1912 state, and opened to the public in 1983. But W. R. Motherwell was more than just a textbook figure with a stern visage. As letters to his children reveal, he was a loving father who openly expressed his affection. During a 1906 Moose Jaw convention, for example, he wrote, "I see a great many sights, meet a great many people, & have a pretty-good time on trips like this, but none of them fills the place of my two pets at home whom I often

Like all homesteads, the Motherwell farm was built on the open prairie. Today, the subsequent landscape improvements stand in stark contrast to the original farmyard. (Parks Canada: *Lanark Place: Memories of an Ontarian West,* p. 12)

long for." In the margin of another 1906 letter is "42 kisses. . . . Is that enough? Well, here is more. . . ."

According to research conducted by Parks Canada, "W. R. Motherwell often stated that he wanted to build a home of which his children would not be ashamed." But the same report suggests, "W. R. Motherwell planned a home that he thought would be fitting of a man in a position of authority and dignity, a home to display an air of refinement and culture as he perceived these on the basis of his rural Ontario background. By standards of the day and the district, the Motherwells' stone home was something more than an average comfortable farm home."

The motives behind the construction of W.R.'s fieldstone home were no doubt mixed, and it is due to the exhaustive Parks Canada research that so much is known about them. For example, files include W.R.'s rudimentary sketch of a house similar to the one he built, drawn while he was a student at the Ontario Agricultural College at Guelph in 1881. There are also photographs of the log home he first built, and the information that he wanted to build his stone house overlooking Pheasant Creek but, thwarted by bureaucracy, had to create his own oasis on the plain.

He began life as the fourth son on a small farm in Lanark County, near Perth, Ontario, and was twenty-two when he filed for his homestead in 1882. Two years later, he married Adeline Rogers, the daughter of a Manitoba homesteader, and they had four children, two of whom survived infancy.

In addition to the demanding work of homesteading, W.R. gathered stones from fields and ravines and, by 1896, was able to have a fieldstone stable built by Adam Cantelon of Lorlie. In 1907, a frame superstructure replaced the roof

to create the barn that still dominates the property.

By April 1897, *The Grenfell Sun* was reporting that "the plans and specifications for a neat residence has [sic] just been completed by Mr. A. M. Fraser, architect. It is the proposed property of Mr. Wm. Motherwell, north of Indian Head, and when completed will cost in the neighbourhood of $4000."

Work on Lanark Place progressed quickly, and by that summer, the fieldstone walls were almost finished. Unfortunately, reported the August 11 edition of *The Vidette,* "Mr. Adam Cantelon, while engaged in building Mr. Motherwell's new house at Abernethy, fell from the second storey on Monday morning and sustained a very bad fracture of the leg which it is feared may lead to the loss of the limb."

Whether Cantelon did lose his leg was not recorded, but the home he built still speaks of his skill and, as illustrated by the stones placed according to colour as well as size and shape, artistry.

The beauty of the coursed stonework is further enhanced by the home's predominantly

Italianate style – square main section, hip roof and ornamental brackets – popular in Ontario in the 1860s, especially in Lanark County. But few prairie homes are pure in style, and the Motherwell house was no exception: the highly decorative bargeboard and finial of the Gothic-style dormer on the rear kitchen suggests High Victorian excess, while the balcony/porch projection at the front is Eastlake in its embellishment.

The highly eclectic home was finished enough for W.R. and Adeline to hold a dinner for twenty-five couples on New Year's Day 1898. Shortly thereafter, the Jan 26, 1898 edition of the *Vidette* listing the "business done by P. Kerr, contractor during 1897 . . .," included "WR Motherwell, stone residence $3,000 . . ."

Adeline succumbed to asthma in 1905 and, after a secret three-year courtship, W.R. married Catherine (Kate) Gillespie, an Ontario-trained teacher who had followed her parents to western Canada and first taught at the Orkney stone school. Her various teaching positions culminated with her role as principal of the File

Hills Residential School, a rare appointment for a woman at the end of the nineteenth century.

After her marriage to W.R., Kate not only presided over the Motherwell household, she was active in various women's associations. Her speeches to them suggest what today would be termed a "feminist" bent.

Kate accompanied W.R. to Ottawa and returned to Lanark Place with him in 1939. When he died four years later, she moved into Abernethy and completed the sale of the farm to W.R.'s grandson, who moved into the house in 1953 and died the same year. Parks

Canada acquired the farm in 1966, the same year the Historic Sites and Monuments Board of Canada recommended that Motherwell be designated a person of national historic significance. The W. R. Motherwell Homestead National Historic Site of Canada, open every day from the May long weekend until Labour Day, commemorates that significance with the restoration of the buildings and, to illustrate Motherwell's practise and promotion of scientific farming methods, the farmstead.

His children would not be ashamed. ❧

Today the restored barn provides a glimpse into the variety of activities that occurred on a prairie farmstead.

Smithfield

THE SMITH FARMHOUSE, NEAR ARCOLA

The history of Smithfield is one of love, lust, land, and loss. In the best fairytale tradition, however, it ends happily. ❧ It begins with the illegitimate birth of James Mitchell Smith in Scotland in 1862. He lived with his mother, Christine Smith, an illiterate linen weaver, until she died three years later. He then lived with his aunt and uncle, Jane and Robert Mitchell, wealthy farmers. ❧ He arrived in the Arcola area in 1891. Living with John McLaren on John's homestead, he staked his own homestead but, after discovering its poor quality, bought land in 1895. ❧ This land had witnessed its own sorrows. In 1882, Alexander McNabb had arrived from Scotland with his wife, Mary Ann, and had filed for a

The wedding photo of James Smith and Betsy Anderson, 1898. Betsy died in 1906, after living at Smithfield for only a few years. (Rick Krehbiel)

homestead and pre-emption in the broad, flat valley at the foot of the Moose Mountains. The following year, Alex and a daughter died, the seventh McNabb child to do so. Mary Ann buried her husband and child on the homestead, the northwest quarter of the half-section claimed by Alex, and, with her two remaining children, continued improving the land.

She was granted the home quarter in 1886 and, by 1890, was ready to start improving the pre-emption, the south-west quarter. By that time, however, Philander Finn had buildings on it, and claimed it as his homestead. Like another, similarly covetous neighbour, he said it had been abandoned.

A Presbyterian minister supported Mary Ann's claim, describing her as a "poor widow of indomitable courage" who "can solder tin-plate when necessary." She had also learned to speak the Assiniboine language "without stuttering." Considering her many talents and the number of times she had "stood on the brink of the grave," he wrote, the government should follow

the Bible's instructions to "Plead for the widow."

Although the Department of the Interior initially listened to the Presbyterian minister, Philander was granted the southwest quarter in 1893. He sold it to James Smith in 1895.

Three years later, James returned to Scotland to marry Betsy Anderson. Four children were subsequently born at Smithfield but, with the birth of the fourth in 1906, Betsy died. James was devastated.

A year before she died, however, the whole family visited Scotland and came back with an extra child: Bruce Anderson Smith, born to Betsy Anderson in 1895 and raised by her parents. The Smiths also returned to Canada with Betsy's niece, seventeen-year-old Betsy Ramsay, who became their domestic help.

Betsy Ramsay married widower James in 1920.

"Old Jimmy Smith ran the farm with the help of his kids until Bruce returned from World War I and took over," explains Rick Krehbiel, the grandson of Bruce, who had moved to the Nipawin area

in 1934. "Jimmy had contracted the Spanish Flu in 1919, and was never strong after that. But, to stop the succession of land out of his blood line, Jimmy married Betsy Ramsay."

When James died in 1928, the family unravelled completely. Betsy maintained the farm with the help of a hired man who had arrived in the district with a questionable history and little respect for anyone else's. He is credited with ploughing over the McNabb graves on the land acquired by James in 1908. When Betsy died in 1971, she left the farm to the hired man, who sold it. Subsequent owners accelerated the decline of Smithfield.

The house at the heart of Smithfield, however, endured.

The exact date of its construction and the name of the man who built it are unknown. Local history has narrowed its completion to around 1903, and Robert McIlvenna of Oxbow is said to have been the stonemason. Given that the stonework is the same as that of neighbouring Restalrig, McIlvenna would seem likely.

The understated Scottish style of Restalrig is even more evident at Smithfield. Simple in its symmetry, the only attempts at artistry are the arches over the windows flanking the front door. It's as if the stonemason, cautioned against any fripperies, surreptitiously slipped in keystones in a barely discernable darker grey. The main entrance was left barefaced, with sidelights and a transom of red and green glass the only deviations from the owners' Calvinistic heritage.

The Smithfield crown jewel was the 1906 barn. Twenty-five metres square, it had three alleys, 5.5-metre-high fieldstone walls, and an elaborate feed system from the loft. It was, as described by Arcola writer Leigh Robinson in a 2006 *Façade* article, "a cathedral of stone with soaring interlocking posts and beams supporting a vast cottage-style roof punctuated by wire-meshed glass skylights."

This monument to both agriculture and the craftsmanship of its unknown builder is now gone, burned and bulldozed by a 1981 owner. The house, abandoned, began to

lose its one-storey stone addition on the north side and fell prey to vandals and the elements.

In 2005, however, something "cosmic" happened, says Rick Krehbiel. A resident of British Columbia, he was attending a family wedding when, during a discussion with his mother's aging cousin, he suddenly became "obsessed" with Smithfield. A month later, he had a leas-

ing arrangement with the owner and had started renovations. He hopes to have it habitable for his retirement.

"My goal is to preserve the house and spend time there. It's a beautiful piece of work. Stunning. And it's part of the family history so it will be a focus for that history. But it wasn't built as a museum. It was built for James and Betsy Smith's descendants. I intend to honour that." ❧

Although the main house is in good repair, the low back addition has started to crumble at the corner.

The Bell Farm

NEAR INDIAN HEAD

The round barn on the Bell farm is not only a Saskatchewan icon, it is celebrated by barn aficionados across North America. 🌿 This fieldstone structure is a vestige of a farm that once covered more than 52,000 acres of land at Indian Head, the Canadian version of the "bonanza farms" established in Minnesota and North Dakota in the 1870s. These models, defined as 3,000 acres or more and made possible by the development of practical farm machinery, copied the techniques of the expanding industrial corporations in the eastern United States. They were also controversial because, due to their large volume of business, the railway, millers and manufacturers favoured them over the small farmers.

A *circa* 1884 view of the stone farmhouse and round barn, two of over one hundred structures erected for Major Bell by A.J. Osment and his construction crew during the first year of operation. (Saskatchewan Archives Board R-A 4900–3)

William Robert Bell, who was born of United Empire Loyalists in Brockville, Ont., became aware of these large agrarian establishments during a farming experience in Minnesota. Shortly after his return to Canada, he took the train from Winnipeg to Brandon, where he set out on foot to view the land through which the Canadian Pacific Railway was to pass. He stopped when he came to what is now Indian Head.

His idea of forming a company, raising funds, and acquiring enough land to establish a large farm came to fruition in the spring of 1882, when the new Qu'Appelle Valley Farming Company Limited acquired about 23,000 acres from the Dominion Government and 29,111 acres from the CPR. The farm encompassed a block of land extending eleven kilometres north and five kilometres south of Indian Head, and Major Bell – a title he acquired during the Fenian Raids – was its general manager.

The breaking of land began immediately and so did the building campaign. As a result, the report to the twenty-four shareholders at the first annual meeting in January 1883 included the following description:

The main farmhouse, 40x34 [12 x 10 m], with wing 23x44 [7 x 13.5 m], is a substantial stone building, two full stories, with 16 rooms, 3 halls, buttery, pantry, 4 closets and cellar, (frost proof) 20x30 [6 x 9 m]. It is finished except some inside painting, and is now furnished throughout and occupied.

The main stable is circular, 64 feet [19.5 m] diameter, built of stone, with cone-shaped roof, surmounted with a lookout tower. The stable contains 2 box stalls and 29 single stalls, stableman's office, oat bin (4000 bush. capacity) with hopper bottom arranged so that the feeding is accomplished in a few moments by one man in attendance; hay loft holding 100 tons.

Two months after this meeting, the company bought the section of land set aside as the site of Indian Head. By the summer of the same year, 160 horses and oxen had broken 6,000 acres, and seventy buildings, including twenty-seven cottages, had been built on various sections. Bell guided operations with a telephone from his office to every cottage and main building, possibly the first rural telephone in the North-West Territories. He also kept fastidious records, but, as pointed out in *Indian Head: History of Indian Head and District,* "His system had one catch; it seldom showed a profit."

Due to low cereal prices, disappointing crops in 1883 and '84, and a substantial outlay of cash to induce squatters to leave company land, some financial obligations were not met. Nonetheless, the Bell Farm remained in an expansionist mode: an Indian Head hotel and grain elevator were built and an agricultural college under the direction of Professor Tanner of England was promised.

In 1885, the North-West Rebellion involved both Bell and his work horses in military transportation. Little land was seeded that year, settlers stayed away because of the unrest, and the CPR continued to pressure Bell for payments that, he stated, were higher than the original agreement.

Refinancing in 1886, as well as the sale of the Indian Head townsite, allowed the Bell Farm to continue under the new name of Bell Farm Company Limited. But the money problems continued and, in April 1888, farm equipment was seized, including 41 binders, 38 seeders, 47 spring tooth harrows, and 38 wagons. According to E. C. Morgan's 1966 exposition in *Saskatchewan History,* "This action was the beginning of the breakup of the Bell Farm Company, which was completed the following year."

Subsequently, writes Morgan, Major Bell entered into "some arrangement with the Company" which allowed him to commence farming on his own 13,000-acre farm in 1888. The Canadian Cooperative Colonization Company Limited acquired much of the remaining original farm.

As an individual farmer, Major Bell had good crops and also the time to indulge in his favourite activities, winning prizes for his marksmanship and heavy draught horses, starring in cricket matches, and presiding over groups such as the Indian Head Liberal Conservative Association. In 1893, however, fire destroyed many of his buildings and stored harvest. A year later, the district suffered the worst crop in its history. In 1895, wheat prices dropped drastically, and his wife died.

Bell's farm animals, buildings, and furniture were auctioned off, and his land was sold the following year. Few locals mourned the loss, most claiming the town and district would benefit from the subsequent establishment of many smaller farms. As the diary of one young farmer stated,

"There is to be a sale of everything. All the farmers are jubilant."

Historians take a different view, most agreeing that the Bell farm was a scheme ahead of its time. And finally, it would appear, others do too. In 2006, the Bell Barn Society of Indian Head was established to ensure that the memory of the Bell farm and the actual stone barn regain

their leading position in Saskatchewan history: the collapsing barn has been dismantled and will be rebuilt to its original 1882 appearance.

It's an outrageous postscript to an outrageous project. Major Bell would approve.

The Bell round barn continues to deteriorate. (Bernard Flaman, Saskatchewan Ministry of Tourism, Parks, Culture and Sport)

The Wright Farmhouse

NEAR BALCARRES

Williliam Henry Wright was thirty-five and unmarried when he built his five-bedroom stone house high on the plain west of Abernethy. According to his descendents, it symbolized his vision of the future in this fertile land. This same vision had inspired his neighbour William Richard Motherwell to build a similarly grand house about eight kilometres to the east, but the Motherwell homestead is now a national historic site, and William's abandoned and vandalized farmhouse is locally famous as the site of spooky scenes in the 2004 movie *Tideland*. ✺ William Wright came from Ontario to the Pheasant Hills district of the North-West Territories in 1891, when his homesteader father,

ABOVE: The oculus – a round window with a single pane of glass – in the triangular pediment is flanked by fish-scale shingles, while ornate brackets support the entire roof over this bay window.

FAR RIGHT: Detail of the stone work. Note the two beige stones on either side of the central bluish stone – two halves of the same rock.

struction of his two-and-a-half-storey stone house. According to the memoir "The Wright Stone House" written by his son, William Russell Wright, the stones were gathered from the surrounding fields by the family.

"A Scottish stonemason by the name of (John) Barnes from Indian Head was employed, and by working with him my father also became very good at cracking, shaping and placing stones," wrote William Russell in 1993. "If you look closely you will notice that all the large stones above all the windows and doors are tapered so that the more weight put on them the tighter they will fit. The stone walls were about two feet thick [half a metre], an air space, then lathe and plaster. The deep windows provided an excellent place for house plants of which my mother,

Gertrude Wright, had many all year."

Carpenter Ed McDamus travelled to Ontario to select the doors, windows, and finishing lumber, such as the ornate brackets under the eaves, the fish-scale shingles in the pediment over the two-storey bay, and inside, the tongue-and-groove wainscoting and window-well linings in the dining room. The attention to detail is apparent in the saw-tooth shapes within the triangle of the two larger brackets on the bay and the matching shapes below the bull's-eye blocks on the corners of the dining room doors, a room still decorated with a nine-foot-high (3 m) tin ceiling.

Besides the spacious parlour, dining room, and hall, the first floor contained a huge kitchen with a pantry and a washroom with its own

George, brought out his wife and eight of his ten children. William, twenty-four years old at the time, took out a loan of one hundred dollars to buy a horse and ox to break the land that same year. With his father and brothers, he harvested the first crops with scythe and sickle.

By 1902, William was able to buy his own half-section of land southwest of his father's homestead and begin con-

exterior doorway. The porch off the front door is original to the house, while a wrap-around porch on the south and west side was added later. One of the second-storey bedrooms opened onto a balcony on the roof of the front porch.

The most uncommon features of the home were its electrical system, which was operated by a generator and sixteen large storage batteries in the basement, and a water pressure system that allowed a bathroom with toilet and clawfoot tub on the second floor. According to William Russell Wright, the water system "required a lot of work pumping up the pressure."

That William Henry was an optimist is unquestionable: his house was completed in 1905, but he did not marry until 1913. His wife, who had settled with her family north of Qu'Appelle in 1885, was first married to William's brother George Leopold, who died of asthma in 1907. William and Gertrude had four children, ideal for the number of bedrooms built so many years before.

About half a kilometre down the road was the 1908 Tipperary School, still standing one hundred years later, and further down the same road the Methodist "Wright's Church." William's sister-in-law Annie Wright was buried from this church before it was completed in December 1905. The church is now gone, but headstones in the adjacent Wright's Cemetery still mark the resting place of other Wright family members and their neighbours.

William's grand home is also just a memory in stone. Over the years, he had purchased additional land locally and elsewhere, and in 1928, he and Gertrude moved to Regina with the intention of retiring. But the 1929 stock market crash and Great Depression changed that plan, and by 1932, they gave up their Regina home and considerable land holdings to return to the stone house. " . . . On their return it was in a sad state of repair, including the electric and water systems which were useless," wrote William Russell. "The depression years of the 1930s made it impossible to restore the house."

Gertrude and William nevertheless farmed from their

Detail of a triangular sawtooth bracket.

stone home until retiring to Indian Head in 1944. Their son Wilfred continued farming from the house until he was killed in a farm accident in the late 1940s. Although still in the family, this stately home has been empty since the 1960s. ❧

Interior view, showing the bull's-eye blocks at the top corners of the door, the pressed tin ceiling, and the wide baseboards.

OPPOSITE: The sole surviving structure of the former Sunbeam Farm, the barn, with its steep gable roof, incorporated large stones at the corners for stability. Two of the three original louvered cupola air vents remain atop the roof.

Sunbeam Farm

THE BRASSEY FARM, NEAR INDIAN HEAD

The small stone horse barn standing alone in a field two and a half kilometres southwest of Indian Head is as quietly unassuming as the prairie itself. Those who know it, however, marvel at its connections with events and people of historical significance. ❧ Originally, the barn was one of several buildings on Sunbeam Farm, which was established under the sponsorship of Lord Thomas Brassey, a man of wide interests and the money to indulge them. In 1876, for example, Lord Brassey and his family set sail in his steam yacht, the *Sunbeam,* and continued their voyages throughout the Pacific Ocean until Lady Brassey died in 1887. ❧ Such adventures were possible because of the wealth of Lord Brassey's

The Sunbeam Farm barn during operation of the farm in 1892. (Albert May)

father, also named Thomas, who built railways across Great Britain and worldwide. One of the largest of these undertakings was Canada's Grand Trunk Railway.

It was this railwayman's eldest son who was elevated to the peerage, however. He was also a Member of Parliament, Governor of Victoria, Australia, and, among many other interests, president of Dr. Barnardo Homes, a charitable organization that sent Britain's surplus children to Canada to provide cheap agricultural and domestic labour. Remarkably, Lord Brassey still had time to pursue his interest in colonizing Canada's North-West Territories.

In September 1887, for example, the "Church Colonization Society," known locally as the Christ Church Settlement, was inaugurated east of Qu'Appelle under the sponsorship of what was generally known as The Brassey Company. The selection of immigrants for this colony, the purchase of a one-mile-square section of land to be divided into forty acres for each family, and the construction of a cottage on each parcel was carried out under the direction of Professor H. Tanner, a British government examiner in agriculture.

The idea behind the Church Colonization Society was to provide a home and employment to English families who, after gaining farming experience, would either take up a free homestead or buy more land. The scheme was short-lived, however, mostly because the settlers soon filed for the free 160-acre homesteads available nearby.

Meanwhile, another colonization venture – the Bell Farm Company – was in financial difficulty, and a Brassey Company subsidiary, the Canadian Co-operative Colonization Company, acquired much of the Bell land. According to the April 20, 1892 *Montreal Gazette,* this subsidiary eventually owned 45,000 acres, with the plan of establishing a series of 2,500-acre subordinate companies. The first of these was the Canadian Alliance Farming Company, under the chairmanship of Professor Tanner, and located south of Indian Head.

By 1891, the Sept. 19 *Manitoba Evening Free Press* announced: "Professor Tanner is completing the arrangements for a second farm of the same size [as the Canadian Alliance Farm] to be put under a complete outfit in the early part of next year. This farm will be known as the Sunbeam Farm, thus making allusion to the priceless sunshine of the North-West, and a name so closely associated with Lord Brassey."

Professor Tanner resigned as chairman of the Canadian Alliance Farming Company in 1892 to become chairman of The Sunbeam Farming Company, Limited. According to the book *History of Indian Head and District,* this farm was the chief centre for the stock-raising ventures and also grew grain "in a large way."

The history book goes on to state, "This was not simply another big farm or a purely large scale land deal. It was based on the idea of bringing settlers out, giving them a brief farming training, establishing them on larger farms, and at the same time providing them with religious and social facilities in close proximity to their farms."

For example, in November 1892, Professor Tanner presented a watercolour picture representing a bird's-eye view of the proposed town of Brassey, to be built opposite Indian Head, south of the CPR track. According to the local newspaper, it showed the proposed town to be "beautifully laid out and to possess a church, parsonage and hospital, fine stores and business blocks and several rows of houses and cottages for those employed on the Estate."

The work on these buildings began in 1894, the same year Lord Brassey finally visited his Indian Head project. When he returned home, according to the local history book, Lord Brassey "devoted his attention primarily to the social and community

requirements of the Indian Head Settlement. He began to dispose of his farms . . . but they were in the hands of the liquidator from 1895." Lord Brassey's explanation for this failure, as quoted in the 1894 Department of the Interior's Annual Report, blames his manager.

His other goal was achieved in 1895, however, when Bishop Burn of Qu'Appelle opened St. John's Anglican Church, built with Lord Brassey's money on the site of the proposed town of Brassey. Immediately southeast of St. John's Church, he constructed and furnished Bishop's Court, a long, three-storey, half-timbered building on a field-stone foundation and bearing a large, carved panel displaying the arms of the Diocese of Qu'Appelle.

But by 1912, Bishop's Court was considered too large and the location of St. John's Church awkward due to trains delaying services. The church was demolished and Bishop's Court, its top two storeys removed and its coat of arms donated to the local museum, eventually became a private home.

Lord Brassey died in 1918, his stone horse barn the only recognizable remnant of his bold – and compassionate – Canadian ventures. Although one of its three cupolas has blown off and its stalls have been removed for the storage of grain, its half-metre thick, cut-stone walls still stand strong and straight. "The rain really brings out their colours," says Albert May with obvious affection. Albert's family owned it for fifty-one years, and the new owner has promised him he would not demolish it. Albert lives by that promise. ❧

TOP: Front of the Sunbeam Farm barn showing the segmented yellow brick arches over the door and window.

BOTTOM: One of three cupolas that served to vent the barn loft.

The Purvis Farmhouse

NEAR CARIEVALE

Uncertainty is the only certainty about the history of Fred and Maggie Purvis's home south of Carievale – other than the evidence of bootlegging and political interference, that is. ❧ Fred's name was entered for a military homestead in 1886, for example, but he was obviously ambivalent about claiming it, as he never appeared on the land until 1891. That he finally obtained title in 1900 is largely due to his father's influence with his Member of Parliament, John Bryson, and the Minister of the Interior after 1888, Edgar Dewdney. ❧ This influence began within a year of Fred and his two brothers filing for the half-section of land, when their father, Dr. George A. Purvis of Portage du Fort, Quebec, began what became nearly a decade of correspondence with Dewdney, Bryson, Department

ABOVE: The year 1903 is painted on a stone between the two arched brick lintels.

BELOW: The addition on the left lacks the symmetrical design of the front of the original house, and displays segmented brick arches above the windows and doorway.

of the Interior officials in Ottawa, and the agent at the nearest Dominion Lands office.

"The boys" – Fred, George, and Herbert – never lifted a finger. And that was the problem. Veterans of the 1885 North-West Rebellion were eligible for 320 free acres, subject to the usual conditions of entry, but it appears that the boys' military bounties were bought rather than earned, and they ignored the requirements for keeping the land.

Finally, an exasperated Department of the Interior official strongly advised Dewdney against more concessions, and the land agent, who had been stalling other entries for the lands in question, was told to protect the lands until May 1, 1891, "but if they fail to comply with above conditions, no further protection will be granted."

Fred, age thirty-three and accompanied by his wife and seven children, eventually showed up and met his homesteading obligations. So did George. There is no local record of Herbert.

Fred, who listed himself as a farmer and miller, built his first house of sod. His second was constructed in two stages, probably because the number of children increased to ten. His decision to build with stone may have been based on the ready availability of material, a condition still apparent today, but it also may be due to his background: Portage du Fort is rich in quarried stone buildings, including Dr. George A. Purvis's historic home on Mill Street.

The history of the home's first half is unknown. Built of granite and sandstone in the rural-Ontario style, with a steep gable over the central front door, it has massive cornerstones but, like all the stones, their irregular cut suggests a stonemason of elementary skill. Even the straight door and window lintels are merely three rough-cut sandstones.

In 1903, the year painted under the end gable, an extension was built perpendicular to the original home. It too had a gable over the main door, but it is a much finer construct, with pastel-pink shades of sandstone on the two sides facing the road.

Local lore has this sandstone imported from Ontario, but it is more likely that the stonemason handpicked these stones nearby. Their careful squaring and neat fit, as well as the precise, curved lintels of brick, indicate just such a meticulous craftsman. No record of his name exists, but it was probably James Greig, who is documented as the builder of the fine 1905 field-stone church in Carievale, and whose name and occupation – "Jas. Greig Builder" – is etched in the 1902 Robert Mann fieldstone house two kilometres north of the Purvis home. The stonework and lintels of the Mann house and Purvis extension are identical.

The contrast between the exterior of the original Purvis house and the extension is as striking inside. As the current owners, the Stanley families, state, "The south end is plain jane," while the north extension is notable for the elaborate woodwork of the staircase and wide arch between the parlour and dining room.

It was from the plain-jane end that old-timers remembered buying "Yankee booze" bootlegged across the international border three kilometres south of the Purvis home during Saskatchewan's prohibition years, 1917–1924. Bob Stanley also tells of the cache of old liquor bottles found under one of the granaries.

Other memories of the Purvis home are more genteel. Mildred Finney, born in 1908,

says her grandmother Maggie Purvis was "good-looking and classy, and that's the way she kept her home. She and grandpa put on a show; they made a lot of money and they spent it."

Perhaps that's why it was Great West Life that sold the farm to Morton Stanley in 1943; Morton's son Bob says the Purvises "lost the farm in the 1930s." The Stanleys subsequently endured their own tragedy, when Bob's thirty-three-year-old mother died from polio. His heartbroken father never entered their bedroom again.

Bob and his family, however, lived in the entire house, and today so do Bob's son and daughter-in-law, Lee and Laura. Interior renovations are ongoing, and there is talk of replacing the veranda torn from the extension by a cyclone. Nobody seems bothered by the ghost Laura swears she saw in the bedroom; "I only saw it once, but you hear things," she says. Everyone just nods. ❧

The original house was perfectly symmetrical, a common feature of many nineteenth-century Ontario homes.

The Stones of Moffat

NEAR WOLSELEY

The 1954 movie *Brigadoon* tells of two American tourists who stumble upon a quaint little Scottish village in the mist, only to discover it reawakens for just one day every hundred years. *Brigadoon* was a love story. ❧ Saskatoon author and artist Kay Parley likens Moffat to Brigadoon. ❧ Moffat is elusive. Settled in the 1880s, it consisted of forty families spread over 92,000 acres south of Wolseley. These families, mostly from the lowlands of Scotland, settled haphazardly along ancient bison trails. According to Kay's love story, *They Cast a Long Shadow,* a standing joke among four generations of Moffatites was that nobody could find it. ❧ The ragged boundaries of the Moffat district were determined by membership in what is still known as Moffat Church. A Dr. Moffat of Scotland owned land

Loganston now stands abandoned, but once was the focal point of the Gibson family's daily life at Moffat.

next to an early settler who not only worked the doctor's land for him but was also under the impression that a portion of it would be donated for the first church. The frame Moffatville Presbyterian Church was erected on that land in 1884. When the misunderstanding became evident, the building was moved and, in 1891, replaced by a new fieldstone edifice called St. Andrew's Presbyterian Church.

Kay, who was born in Moffat in 1923, describes St Andrew's as "an unpretentious church, in simple Presbyterian style, durable and functional." A United Church since 1925, weekly services have continued in it for more than one hundred years. Kay's 1965 book offers one of the reasons

for this devotion: "Moffat Kirk [the Scottish Presbyterian word for church] is only 76 years old, but, to the descendants of the Scottish pioneers, the stones of Moffat are much older than that. They are, in a sense, the stones of Scotland, part of a tradition that goes back to antiquity."

The kirk was not the only example of that tradition. Today, five stone houses are still standing, but at one time within the districts of Moffat and the neighbouring Greenville, there were twelve homes, two churches, and a school of fieldstone.

Kay's love of these homes began in the one her grandfather built, but her appreciation of their style began with her visit to Scotland. A Scottish house, she writes, is based on the Scots' sense of thrift: they use the materials at hand, which results in homes that "seem to grow from the earth of which they are so much a part . . ."

Canadian prairie dwellers, living with subtle colour, can appreciate quiet colours too. It is all there, in our native field-stone: warm rose, burnished yellow, soft browns, touch of sober green, glistening here and there with the salt-cake purity of mica. The immigrant stonemasons, by following their own tradition, captured the natural colouring of Moffat.

Three Scottish stonemasons settled in Moffat. One of them, William Gibson, arrived in 1883 with wife Margaret and five children, and was the first to build a stone house (1884/85.) He called it Loganston, but few remember and no one seems to care. The two other experienced stonemasons were William McCall, who arrived in 1884 with his wife, Jane, and grown family, and John Hutson, who married McCall's sister Ann and arrived in 1885. Shortly thereafter, they built their stone homes, identical in their symmetry, only a short footpath apart.

Although both the Hutson and McCall homes are now demolished, several of the stone houses they built for others are still standing. Craig-farg, for example, was built for Daniel and Margaret Ferguson

FARMHOUSES & BARNS   33

and their ten children, who arrived in the 1880s. It was sold in 1968 by the youngest son, and is now empty.

Daniel Ferguson's third son, Peter, had a stone house built for him by Hutson in the 1890s. Called Berryhill, it is the smallest of the stone houses; Kay calls it a "fairy house." It is now owned by descendants of Daniel's extended family and serves as the children's summer playhouse.

Hutson and McCall also built a fieldstone house for Walter and Jane Scott, who arrived with their seven children in 1886. In recent years, the Walter Scott house stood alone and crumbling on a rise above Kenny's Lake (one of the many Moffat sloughs called lakes because of their size), and was totally demolished in 2007.

In 1892, Kay's grandfather, Robert Parley, built Hayfield. He had left Scotland in 1882, but returned three years later to bring back Moffat's first bride, Mary Agnes. His square, two-storey home fulfilled her one desire: a bay window, the only bay window of stone in the community.

Another stone house built by its owner is Ladybank,

completed by Francis Pow in 1893. He arrived in Moffat in 1885, bringing with him his wife, Jessie, their six children, and his Glasgow shipbuilding skills. His vandalized home still stands on a knoll overlooking Kindred's Lake.

In 1903, Francis helped one of his sons, James, build a stone house down the road. Its most impressive features are the immense red sandstone lintels above the first-

floor doors and windows. It is still owned and used by a direct descendant.

Kay's book includes a Moffat map but, to discover the stones of Moffat, it's best to take her advice: "Moffat, Assiniboia, North West Territories, was a kind of Brigadoon and, like the wanderers of the musical *Brigadoon,* you'll have to lose yourself a while in order to go there . . . like Brigadoon, Moffat exists in time. . . ." ❧

The Gibson family, photographed on their farm at Moffat, south of Wolseley. (Saskatchewan Archives Board R-B 2748–2)

St. Andrew's Presbyterian Church, erected in 1891.

The Parker Farmhouse

NEAR CARDROSS

I t's a lonely and strangely beautiful land near the northern tip of the Missouri Coteau. ❧ *Coteau* is a French word for an elevated geographical feature such as a plateau, so the highway south from Moose Jaw rises to a hilly plain of scrubby grasses interrupted by cultivated fields sometimes so stony one can only marvel at the life force of plants. Every once in a while, seeking shelter in a draw, there's a small frame farmhouse, its out-buildings clustered close. ❧ But then, three kilometres west of Cardross and still standing proud on the highest rise in the area, is William Edward (Eddie) Parker's fieldstone farmhouse. The sight is as marvelous as the blades of wheat pushing past the stones. ❧ Eddie was one of eight boys born and raised on a farm in bush country near Peterborough, Ontario. He arrived

The cobblestone pattern on the north and west sides are the work of Eddie Parker.

in Saskatoon to work on one of the iron bridges in 1906, but returned home when he contracted typhoid fever. In 1910, he came west again, this time to homestead near Cardross. Six of his brothers followed him.

Eddie's brother Herbert farmed across the road, Louie ranched near Lake of the Rivers, and Alfred was killed in a farming accident. Barkley took over the general store at Cardross, Stanley left for the States, and Charlie returned to stonemasonry like his stay-at-home brother Henry. Charlie and Henry had learned their trade from their mother's brothers, who had trained in Aberdeen, Scotland.

By 1917, Eddie was ready to build his house. According to his daughter, Evelyn McAdam, his brother Charlie is responsi-

ble for the design: reminiscent of a side-gabled Craftsman house, the principal façade is dominated by a deeply sloping roof inset with a gabled dormer and terminating over an open veranda supported by slender wooden piers.

The Craftsman style was inspired by the work of two California architects around 1903 and was popularized throughout North America by magazines, pattern books, and even the catalogues for pre-fab houses. While these may have been Charlie's inspiration, the slightly off-centre vestibule suggests he used the Craftsman concept rather than a pattern for the design.

Equally impressive and just as interesting is the stonework. First, there are two square, obviously deliberate holes in the south wall. "They were for the cooling cupboard but all they did was let in the cold and mice," explains Evelyn. "They weren't such a good idea."

Even more curious is the difference in the stonework. The stones of the east and south sides, which can be viewed from the road, are squared, laid in neat courses,

Detail of the fireplace designed and built by Charlie Parker.

and framed with raised joints. Each first-storey lintel is a long rectangular fieldstone with squared corners, while the stones over the two basement windows have been cut on an angle, with the keystone a perfect triangle. These walls, as well as the precisely laid fireplace in the parlour, were built by Charlie.

The other two sides were built by Eddie, and the contrast is striking. Except for some of the cornerstones, none of the stones have been shaped, and their sizes vary widely. All have been laid in the random rubble style, creating a cobblestone effect. All but one lintel are of multisized stones placed on their small ends. The only similarity with the other two walls is the concrete sills.

Herbert had hauled these stones with horses and a stoneboat from the banks of Lake of the Rivers six kilometres to the west, while Barkley did the carpentry.

The house was finished in 1918, but before Eddie could marry his Ontario fiancée and carry her over its threshold, she died in the flu epidemic of 1919. In January 1923, when

he was almost forty, he married Edith Sunaman, a Crane Valley woman who had come west with her parents. She was twenty-two.

Eddie and Edith had seven girls, the last one born when Eddie was sixty. About that same time, Evelyn left home to join the Royal Canadian Air Force, Women's Division, so, because she and her oldest sister had been driving the tractor and the combine, Eddie rented out the land. Eventually, he and Edith spent the winters in town and, by the early 1970s,

the house was left empty. The farm was sold shortly after Edith died in 1995.

Today, the stones enclose the family home as tightly as they did the day they were laid, but the only sound is the eerie beat of a cardboard label flapping in the wind that fingers an open shed, sighs through the tamaracks, and bends the tall, whispering grasses.

Or, as Evelyn says, "That big old house is sad. It needs to be full of people. It's weeping." ❧

At first glance, the house appears to be symmetrical; however, the entry is offset from the centrally positioned gable window.

The Goodwin House

SASKATCHEWAN LANDING

Surrounded by the hills of the sweeping South Saskatchewan River Valley and standing alone near the broad expanse of Diefenbaker Lake, Goodwin House at Saskatchewan Landing appears small and, with traffic raging by on the adjacent highway, of little significance. But Goodwin House is not what it seems. ❧ The plentiful artifacts in the area, for example, trace a long Aboriginal history, and Don McGowan's *Grass-land Settlers* tells of their establishment of a ferry service at the point where they had previously forded the river. This service became lucrative after the 1882 arrival of the Canadian Pacific Railway in Swift Current, when the easiest access to Battleford was directly north from Swift Current. ❧ With the advent of the North-West Rebellion in 1885, the Battleford Trail became a

The triple gables over the upper-floor windows are unusual features for Saskatchewan architecture.

army at the battlegrounds.

Although the cessation of hostilities reduced traffic on the Battleford Trail, the Landing remained busy and, in 1888, a post office was established under the name "Saskatchewan Landing." Two years later, however, Saskatoon replaced Swift Current as the nearest railway point to Battleford, and the trail emptied.

But one man remembered. Frank Goodwin, a North-West Mounted Police member stationed at Swift Current and involved in the North-West Rebellion, had left the force in late-1885 to marry Mary Rutherford, daughter of a CPR locomotive engineer. They lived in Swift Current until 1900, when they moved into the fieldstone house they had built about a kilometre southeast of the Saskatchewan Landing ferry.

The house took at least two years to build. In May 1898, the *Medicine Hat Times* reported, "Mr. Frank Goodwin is building a ranch at the Saskatchewan Landing," and, in October the next year, it noted, "Sherwood's mason outfit left Maple Creek on Friday night for Swift Current

where they will build a house for Frank Goodwin."

According to accounts by Margaret Noble, a former resident of the house, the basement was dug by Aboriginal men with picks and shovels, and a Métis man named LaRocque built a kiln to reduce limestone to lime f or mortar by burning it for sixty consecutive days. Noble reported that horse, antelope, and deer hair was gathered and added to the lime-sand mixture to stabilize it.

The main entrance faced the water, northward under three gabled dormers. But, although the home's Georgian proportions suggest its classic references, the surrounding open and closed verandas marked it as a ranch home, and the family of ten used the south entrance in the summer kitchen, a one-storey addition to the original house.

About three years after the house was completed and the ranching operation established, hundreds of homesteaders began trekking into the country north of Saskatchewan Landing. They were often forced to wait for a safe crossing by ferry or ice so,

critical conduit for troops and supplies. For example, in mid-April at the Landing, as it was then called, 745 men and 450 horses were transported across the river, where they then continued north to reinforce Major-General Middleton's

according to local accounts, the Goodwin home became a halfway house offering shelter and even meals for families and their animals. Mary also fed the two NWMP who lived in a nearby shack, and eventually opened a store in the summer kitchen.

The Goodwins' hospitality was known far and wide. Dances, card parties, and, when the Anglican priest from Maple Creek arrived, monthly church services were held in the house. The nearby river crossing, with ferry cables snapping, wagons breaking through the ice, and eventually, a "hair-raising" horse-powered cable-car system that floated passengers over the water, provided ongoing excitement.

Art and Besse Smith, Margaret Noble's parents, bought the Goodwin home in 1928 and established an irrigated market garden along the river. The house continued as a social focus, as well as the location of a store and the post office that had transferred from the ferry house to the Goodwin home in 1926.

The Smiths left the stone house in 1949, just before the greatest spectacle since the Rebellion: a concrete and steel bridge was officially opened by the provincial government in June 1950. The following spring it was taken down by rampaging water and ice.

Ferries were returned to service, and a longer, higher bridge was built to accommodate the river that became Lake Diefenbaker after the construction of the Gardiner Dam downstream. Meanwhile, the land on which the stone house stands was sold to the Prairie Farm Rehabilitation Administration (PFRA) in 1959, in preparation for flooding by the proposed dam.

In 1973, 5,534 hectares surrounding Goodwin house became Saskatchewan Landing Provincial Park. The house, still stable on its 1.2 metre-wide fieldstone foundation but its verandas gone and its interior filthy with wildlife dung, was a desolate sight until a late-1980s structural analysis revealed its sturdy condition. The exterior was subsequently restored to its 1915 appearance, while its interior was renovated as a visitor orientation centre and park administration offices.

ABOVE: The iron cresting on the roof and the wrap-around veranda are attractive features on the stone farmhouse.

Today, as yesterday, Goodwin House welcomes travellers. Artifacts and information then entice them to leave for the paths into the surrounding hills and coulees. Some paths lead to more stones: a ceremonial circle, a survey mound, or the remains of a Métis hillside home. Their stories are even older than those of the house below, and in the quiet, they are told. ❧

BELOW: A view from the southeast of the Goodwin house in 1905. (Saskatchewan Archives Board R-A 2279)

Restalrig

THE MCLAREN FARMHOUSE, NEAR ARCOLA

estalrig, despite the vines clawing at its face, grasses pushing against its front door, and trees nudging, shouldering, and scraping, retains its dignity. Solid, symmetrical, and Scottish in its reserve, its presence is undiminished by time. ❧ The original Restalrig is in Scotland, a village now part of Edinburgh and the birthplace of John Peter McLaren. John Peter was a railway engineer who immigrated to the United States and eventually took a job with the Canadian Pacific Railway in Winnipeg, arriving there in 1889. When he discovered he had to wait six weeks to start work, he decided to visit his cousin Scotty Bryce in the North-West Territories. ❧ Scotty, a native of Doune, Scotland, and an agriculture graduate of the University of Edinburgh, had arrived at Cannington Manor in 1882 to teach farming to

A light keystone forms the central stone of the arch over this window.

the young Englishmen, but had soon left to establish a homestead northwest of Arcola.

Despite John's first-hand observation of Scotty's homesteading hardships – as compared to the homesteading glories promised by immigration posters and brochures – he decided to homestead as

well. But his first two attempts in the Moose Mountains northwest of Arcola ended poorly, and the third placed him on a slope of sand and gravel camouflaged by prairie grasses. After the first few furrows, he realized his mistake. Still, the homestead was adjacent to the half-section of land he'd bought in the fertile flat of the broad valley below, so he persuaded the government to let him keep it without the required cultivation.

"And it was on this homestead land that he built a log-and-mud shack at the top of the hill where the wind was good," reports John's grandson Bob McLaren, poking a bit of fun at his grandfather. Bob

now farms that land and knows it and the wind intimately.

By 1895, the rich valley bottom had fulfilled its promise, and John went back to Scotland to marry Joan Turnbull and bring her back to the farm he called Restalrig. Three years later, a new home was built, this time at the bottom of the slope.

The man John hired to build his fieldstone home, Robert (Bob) McIlvenna, had trained as a stonemason near Toronto, but he arrived in the Oxbow area in 1882 as a homesteader. He (and later he and his son Bill) is responsible for many of the fieldstone buildings in southeast Saskatchewan, including the Beckton house at Cannington.

The home Bob McIlvenna built for the McLarens illustrated his training and experience. Each of the squared stones, most of which are of the same width from the top of the two-storey house to the bottom and from corner to corner, were laid in a coursed style that he highlighted with neat white lines. He reserved his artistic touches for the lin-

When completed, Restlarig graceously overlooked the surrounding landscape, with the Moose Mountain hills in the background. A delicately designed front veranda significantly enhanced the stark massing of the house. (Library and Archives Canada: PA-021651)

tels of the second-storey double windows, where he shaped burgundy stones to place as the keystone or to symmetrically flank this centre piece.

Completing this fine home was a shallow hip roof with cresting and wide Prairie-style eaves, and a Victorian-style open porch at the front door.

Descendents recall few interior details other than the master bedroom on the main floor and a separate second-floor bedroom and staircase for the hired help. Also the plumbing: copper vats near the ceiling of the second floor stored water hand-pumped up from the well. The water then flowed by gravity through taps and toilet, rare luxuries at the time. Waste water was directed into a four-compartment septic tank under the front porch.

In 1902, the stone walls of a grand barn were built for the McLarens by a stonemason remembered by the family as Dan Davis (or Davies) of the Carlyle district.

Stonemasons were in demand in the Arcola area as the nineteenth century drew to a close and, with great optimism, the twentieth century began. At least three other

large fieldstone houses were constructed in the lee of the Moose Mountains, including Doune Lodge, the house and barn built for Scotty Bryce by stonemason William Anderson of Arcola.

Doune Lodge remained in the hands of Scotty's direct descendants until 2001, and Restalrig is still owned by the McLaren family. John McLaren sold it to his only son, John, in 1921, and John sold it to the youngest of his

seven children, Bob, in 1960. Bob hopes his oldest son, who bought Doune Lodge, will also take over Restalrig when the time comes.

"You should be prosecuted for child abuse if you give a child a farm today," he says, referring to the economic situation in rural Saskatchewan. "But Restalrig has been in the family for three generations, and I hope it continues into the future. There's some family pride involved." ✽

The stone barn on the McLaren farm supports a high-pitched roof-loft structure, with board and batten gable ends.

OPPOSITE: A massive monument to both the owner and the stonemason who built it, the Powell farmhouse has stood imposingly in a farmyard northeast of Sheho for over a hundred years.

The Powell Farmhouse

NEAR SHEHO

I's a great story: the one about Captain John Powell and his wife, Caroline, building a hotel on the edge of Sheho Lake in anticipation of the arrival of the Canadian Pacific Railway from Yorkton, forty kilometres to the southeast. But the railway was laid three kilometres south and, in the words of the local history book, *They Came From Many Lands,* the hotel became "a symbol of a pioneer's frustrated hopes and dreams." ❧ Is the story true? Only John and Caroline know for sure, but they're buried in a nearby field. If the canola isn't too high, their gravestones can be seen from the front door of their alleged hotel. ❧ The facts as their hired man's son tells them still make a good story, however. It begins in 1890, when the first settler in the Sheho district arrived from North Dakota. Captain A. Holmes was among

Two elaborate tombstones mark the final resting places of the Powell family members.

rose-coloured stone was so large it was split to form the lintels of three windows.

A fieldstone chicken house with a wooden granary above, and a long fieldstone barn with a pole-and-straw roof were built into a bank sloping towards the lake. The chicken house still stands, but part of the barn has crumbled. The gable ends of the fieldstone smokehouse have fallen, but one half, the scalding room, still contains a concrete firebox with a one-metre-diameter cast-iron cauldron sunk into its top, and the other half still has meat hooks screwed into the smoke-blackened ceiling beams.

Although the Powells had no children, the Captain was chairman of the Sheho Lake School, which was on their land, and the school documents add to local stories of his irascible temperament. For example, a letter to the Department of Public Instruction from the secretary treasurer of the school district, dated 1899, states, " . . . this man Powell intends fencing this half section where the school house now stands and is going to forbid the children from going in

those who followed in 1895, filing for a homestead on the land where the Powell house now stands. But he left the following year, returning to the Great Lakes and trading his land for the naval interests of Captain John Powell, who immediately came west to claim his land. Accompanying the short, stocky fifty-year-old was his thirty-six-year-old wife, "a big German woman" who had been his ship's cook.

By 1897, the Powells had local men digging an eight-foot-deep (2.5 m) basement with picks and shovels, hauling

stones on a stoneboat drawn by four horses, and operating a lime kiln, all under the direction of Nels Holor Neilson, who had built the Orkney church and school thirty kilometres to the southeast.

Although the square, two-storey Powell house and its rear extension is bigger than the Orkney school and church put together, Neilson's random rubble style is apparent in all. The stones of the Orkney buildings, however, are unremarkable in size, while the cornerstones and lintels of the Powell house are massive; one

. . . He has also demanded rent for three years for the school house being on his land." A subsequent letter from the department warned the Captain that such actions would result in "serious consequences," but, five years later, accusations were still flying back and forth. The school was finally "disorganized" in 1913, a year after the Captain died.

Caroline carried on the cattle operation after his death. In her company was Gussie Messingchuck, a local Ukrainian girl who had arrived in the house at an unknown date, but who was included in family photographs from the early 1920s. Her 1926 gravestone next to the marker for John and Caroline notes her age as twenty-five and her status as "beloved daughter of Mrs. C. F. Powell."

It was Manfred Hart who met Gussie's body at the train when it was returned home after her death – from diphtheria, he said – in Saskatoon. Manfred had arrived from England to work in the district as a harvester and, in the late fall of 1923, heard that Caroline was looking for someone to care for her cattle while she

and Gussie wintered in California. He worked for Caroline, living above the kitchen, for the next thirteen years.

According to Manfred, "If you treated [Caroline] fair, she'd be fair to you. But if you crossed her, look out." He told his son of a hot summer day when she and he were pitching hay and a life-insurance salesman came along. The salesman ignored her request to remove himself, so she jumped off the stack and said, "Get moving or I'll run you through with this fork." The salesman left.

Caroline died in 1936, her name added to John's anchor-inscribed stone in the field, and left the house and land to Manfred. He promptly married, cleared much of the land to diversify into grain farming,

The stone ruins of the Powell barn stand near the lake that bordered the farm.

and until 1949, raised his family in the big stone house. They returned every summer until the 1970s.

Today, although one corner has fallen away, the house is still impressive. It looms above a sea of grass waving over the skeleton of a long, metal-clad rowboat. The whistle of the train as it passes through Sheho can be faintly heard, but the six pelicans that return every year to the Captain's lake pay it no mind. ❧

View of the Powell farmhouse through the ruins of the barn foundation.

OPPOSITE: The Webster farmhouse is fairly typical of the challenge to preserve historic integrity while accommodating new technology and the need to keep these old farm homes viable in a very different era. Few have been able to achieve the sensitive balance that is evident at this farm.

Granite Lodge

THE WEBSTER FARMHOUSE, NEAR WELWYN

When Alex and Margaret Webster planned their fieldstone house in 1904, they weren't looking for fancy. A simple four-square suited them just fine, stained-glass panels in three windows their one concession to frivolity. It had to be sturdy, however, and big enough to accommodate a family of nine. ✕ Their insistence on these basic qualities has proven to be as important as it was prescient: their son William and his wife, Agnes, had four children and inherited the house in 1941; one of those four children, Della, married Wilson Crosson, had seven children, and assumed ownership in 1973; and the Crossons' son Will and his wife, Sue, became residents in 1996 and are raising their five children under the original galvanized metal roof. Alterations have been carried out with every

Segmented arches have been used throughout this building.

As might be suspected, Alex and Margaret's no-frills attitude had Scottish roots: Alex's Webster grandparents came to Canada from Inverary, Scotland, in the mid-1800s and settled around Owen Sound, Ontario. His father married a Scottish-Canadian girl, and they homesteaded as well. But the land was poor, so in 1882, Alex and his two brothers took the train to Manitoba, boarded a boat for the trip up the Assiniboine River to Fort Ellice, and walked over fifty kilometres west to establish homesteads about twenty kilometres north of Moosomin. A year later, they were joined by their parents, who also filed for a homestead, and their younger siblings.

Alex and Margaret, a schoolteacher and daughter of other homesteaders, raised their seven children in a sod house that, by 1904, was more than a little cramped. So they had Alex Fleming, a Tantallon carpenter who had moved to Regina, draw up plans and estimates of material for a six-bedroom house with half-metre-wide stone walls.

Although the surrounding land does not appear stony,

Will Crosson reports a rocky base in the "runs," the areas not overlaid by several metres of topsoil. Because the same topography exists for kilometres around, three homesteaders in the district hired stonemason "Mr. Chilton" to build their homes at the same time. He and his four helpers would build walls about half a metre high at one house, then move on to the next while the mortar dried.

The Webster foundation was raised in 1905, the house was finished the following year, and Alex and his sons built the fieldstone summer kitchen on the north side the year after that. The massive cornerstones and the random-rubble-style walls were all of granite, which suggested the name of the home, Granite Lodge. The windowsills were concrete and the slightly arched lintels were of concrete blocks.

The interior features included a dumbwaiter from the basement to the pantry, a flour chute from the attic to the pantry – grain was hauled to Moosomin for milling and returned in hundred-pound (45 kg) sacks, which were

change in ownership, but none has involved stability; the house is as straight and intact as the day it was built.

stored in the attic – and a back staircase that Della reports was "excellent for hide and seek." All are gone now, as is the summer kitchen, replaced by a frame addition.

About the same time as the stone kitchen came down, a shelterbelt was planted around the entire yard site. By 2006 the evergreens had formed a long, dignified avenue leading to the house, which itself had taken on new grace. In 2001, the superficial layer of mortar, originally scored with white lines around each stone, was replaced to show more of the granite, and the crumbling concrete windowsills were replaced with flat fieldstones. The lintels were also replaced with fieldstone.

The most obvious change was the addition of an open, two-storey porch at the front entrance. An upstairs exterior door had never led anywhere but straight down – Della had used it to shake her mop – so Will and Sue scanned magazines and the façades of other old houses until they eventually fell in love with a spindled porch on an older home in Brandon and modified the style for their own use.

A century later, the house is fully surrounded by hedges and trees that form part of the shelterbelt.

Walking around the manicured yard to point out this and other cosmetic changes of the recent past and near future, Will reveals his Scottish heritage when he concludes his explanations with understated feeling, "There's a bit of sentiment here." ❧

The Webster farmhouse was clearly intended to have a front veranda, as is evident by the second-storey door leading nowhere. That was only added decades later by the Crosson family. (Della Crosson)

OPPOSITE: The front of the Le Grand farmhouse displays a clean, symmetrical design, and would present a dramatic change from the original wood siding applied to this building.

The Le Grand Farmhouse

NEAR TURTLEFORD

Always possessed of a lively intellect and a curiosity about the world, Marie Le Grand's imagination was immediately fired by her brother's stories of western Canada: the rolling bushland so foreign to one who'd lived all her life on the coast of Brittany, and life in a wild new land so much more exciting than that of a baker's wife in the ancient French town of Quimper. ❧ "My mother's brother and my father's brother-in-law came out here first and went back to brag about all the land in this god-forsaken country," explains Marie's youngest daughter, Genevieve Etcheverry. "So mother was most enthused about coming to Canada. It wasn't what she expected, but she couldn't complain because she was the one who wanted to come here." ❧ Genevieve's older sister, Denise Schmitz, continues: "Mother came

A large dormer window provided additional light to the upper level. The stonemason added a concrete string course at the second floor level to help visually separate the two levels.

from northwest France, right by the sea. The houses were all built of stone. So, when she arrived here and was so lonely and longing for home, she wanted a stone house. There is nothing like a stone house."

Marie waited twenty-three years for her stone house.

Jean Le Grand gave up his Brittany bakery in 1910, and with their two-year-old and a five-month-old, he and Marie immigrated to Wakaw to spend a year with relatives before moving on to homestead land located about

twenty-five kilometres from each of Turtleford, Paradise Hill, and St. Walburg.

As a baker with three years of military experience, Jean knew nothing about farming. But, working long hours with his oxen and horses, and travelling two days to deliver the fruit of his labour, he earned enough to support eight children, build a frame house with a much-coveted bay window, and donate land for a school. He also punched down the bread dough.

It was just as important and, in the early years, as dif-

ficult to meet the family's spiritual needs. At first the occasional priest would say mass in various homes. In 1913, a Roman Catholic church was built twenty-five kilometres away. Finally, in 1924, St. Pierre's Church, now relocated to Paradise Hill and famous for its Berthold Imhoff paintings, was built just eleven kilometres from their home. It was valued for its proximity, not its paintings.

The community was of mixed ethnic roots, and the Le Grands entered into all the activities. But French was always spoken at home: "And it was French French, not French Canadian," says Genevieve firmly. "We did not make pea soup and tourtière either."

In 1933, after many family members had grown up and moved away, Marie's stone house was finally built. A large kitchen was added to the back of the original frame house, and the whole building was veneered with fieldstone from the Le Grand stone piles. These stones were cut but not squared, then each was tightly fitted into irregular spaces in the walls to create a mosaic pattern. The stonemason made concrete blocks to quoin all the corners, frame the windows and doors, and separate the first and second level with a string course.

That stonemason was Karl Gortzyk. According to writer/researcher Ewald Gossner, Karl had arrived from Germany in 1927, and according to Genevieve, "He was a nice fellow. I'd hurry home from school so I could talk to him. We sat outside while he taught me to count to ten in German . . . He taught my brother John how to cut and lay stones. It took them from early spring till late fall to complete the house."

And, Denise reports, "Mother was happy she had a stone house."

Marie and Jean retired to St. Walburg in the mid-1950s, about the same time as Karl returned to East Germany to live with his niece. Two of the Le Grand sons took over the eleven quarters of land Jean had acquired over the years, and sold them in 1973. The home, so loved by Marie and so admired by their neighbours the Roussels that Karl Gortzyk was hired to build them a stone house too, has been empty ever since.

"I'm not sentimental about things like that, but I'm sorry to see it empty with birds flying in and out," says Denise. Having heard reports of its desolation, Genevieve refuses to go and see it at all. ❧

Bay windows have been popular architectural features for centuries, and provide extra interior space as well as attractive exterior building elements.

The use of a bright white mortar, as well as white-painted concrete quoins, are trademark features of stonemason Karl Gortzyk, and may reflect a favourite technique of his German origin. Few other buildings in Saskatchewan display this particular characteristic.

Paisley Farm

THE MCLEAN FARMHOUSE, NEAR ELLISBORO

Harmony of nature's work with that of humans is seldom as realized as it is at Paisley Farm in the Qu'Appelle Valley. The first of these – the foot of a treed ravine opening onto the meandering Qu'Appelle River, about twenty kilometres north of Wolseley – was no accident. It was chosen by Robert McLean after several years of freighting between two Hudson's Bay Company trading posts, Fort Qu'Appelle and Fort Ellice, located near the meeting of the Qu'Appelle and Assiniboine rivers. Robert said it was the finest homesteading land between Winnipeg and the Rockies. He knew what he was talking about. Robert was born in Paisley, Scotland, and twelve years later, after his father died at a relatively young age, he immigrated to the Ottawa area with his family, where he was

The newly completed stone house serves as a backdrop for a group photo. Unlike many houses of this size, this structure sported a very small porch; but its design was delicate compared with the overall massing of the house. (Verna Betker)

soon working in the sawmill industry. In 1876, he joined the North-West Mounted Police and was immediately posted at Fort Walsh, where he was a dispatch rider between the fort and Wood Mountain. He later rode at Major Walsh's right side to attend him during his conferences with Sitting Bull.

By 1879, Robert obtained his discharge from the NWMP and took up freighting with a train of thirty ponies and

carts. Robert knew horses – "McLean had the greatest powers of endurance in the saddle of any man I have every known," said one of his Fort Walsh contemporaries – and he knew what he needed to settle down: water, wood, and a fine hay meadow.

He squatted in the midst of these three necessities in 1881 and filed for a homestead the next year, cutting logs in the ravine for the house he built at the same time. Three other former NWMP also filed for homesteads in the area around what eventually became known as Ellisboro. In 1884, Robert married Quebec-born Isabella Thompson, whose family had settled west of Ellisboro, and the first of their four children was born a year later, shortly after Robert returned from trans-

porting supplies during the North-West Rebellion.

By 1902, the little log house was crowded, so the construction of a more commodious home began with the gathering of stones from the surrounding hills. Many of these, the limestones, were burned for seventy watchful hours in pits fueled by logs from the hills to produce lime for the mortar. It is the story of every stone building of that era, another reason for the affection and reverence they inspire in their families, congregations, and even strangers.

The man who put the stones together at Paisley Farm, John Jamieson, remains a loose sketch only. One local history describes him as Scottish, and another tells of him fashioning a headstone from local granite for the infant son of Ellisboro's Presbyterian minister during the same years the McLean house was being built. He also chewed tobacco, a memory that remained vivid for one McLean who was spattered more than once while he worked below.

The pride John Jamieson took in his work, however, is clearly portrayed by a story in

The datestone located over the front door is hidden from view by the intricate porch, and comes as a pleasant surprise as you enter the house.

the 1966 local history *Man! Man! Just Look at that Land* by Angelina Campbell: "While this house was being erected stone by stone, the owner was asked by G. P. Campbell how the work was coming along. 'Slow, slow,' was the reply. G. P. Campbell, who judged his own masonry as fair, said, 'Perhaps I should come up and give him a hand.' 'Well,' was the considered and flavoured reply, 'He might let you work on the back but I'm bloody well sure he'll never let you work on the front.'"

This careful craftsmanship is still evident. Laid in a coursed-rubble style, each stone is framed with incised lines, and every corner, door, and window has limestone quoins of approximately the same size. The sills are broad bands of limestone, while the massive limestone lintels, some of which are decidedly pink, were shaped to curve gently over every window on both levels. The year 1904 is carved in limestone over the front door.

Long before the stone house was built for his growing family, Robert McLean was also ensuring their educa-

tion as a founding member of the nearby school board, a position he held for thirty-seven years. His descendants are equally proud of the swashbuckler who bought an "Indian pony" for $2, named him Two Dollars, rode him without saddle or bridle in the annual Wolseley Sports Day, and, though nobody bet on the unknown horse, easily won. Thirty minutes after crossing the finish line, the pony stopped running.

Horses and family are still important in this valley home. When the youngest McLean

son married in 1921, Robert and Isabella moved into a smaller home on the property and the younger McLeans raised their four daughters in the stone house. In 1961, they sold it to Bob and Norma Watson, both well-known for their horsemanship. Under the name Steel Thorn Ranch, the Watsons are now partners in the horse-and-cattle operation with their son and his wife, who live in the stone house. And above a space filled by three small bicycles at the back door is a sign: "Reserved for Cowboys." ❧

The segmented stone arches and windowsills are readily discernable, as are the substantial cornerstones. Although the walls are made of various-sized fieldstones, some effort has been made to give them a coursed rather than random pattern, particularly by scoring the mortar joints in a rectangular pattern.

The Stevenson Farmhouse

NEAR VICEROY

When you're 101 years old, it's easy to forgive everyone, even your mother-in-law. And so it was with the late Betty Stevenson when asked about reports that Mary Stevenson was not a favourite with her neighbours. ❧ "Mary was very quick-tempered, and she could be hurtful," agreed Betty. "But people had to get to know her. If you were a bachelor girl and running a boarding house till you were in your forties . . ." ❧ Besides, it couldn't have been easy being married to Robert Stevenson, a Scot who was so frugal that he set his own broken leg and walked with a limp ever after. The neighbours' stories that Mary washed clothes in the big slough out front were also true, but Betty said that was because Robert and Mary had no well during their early homesteading years.

The bay window displays the mixture of stone and concrete used for this house.

in 1906. His father, Robert, was a butcher and his mother, Grace, died at his birth. Robert, heartbroken, left for Canada the following year.

On his way to Edmonton, Robert stopped at Moose Jaw, where he met Mary, ten years his senior, and took a job as a butcher. In September 1908, he applied for a homestead entry sixteen kilometres northwest of Viceroy. Betty said that his three boys were brought to Canada by his two sisters, and homestead records show that the family of five was living in a sod-and-frame house by 1909.

Robert, however, wanted a stone house. Not only did it remind him of home, the material was free. He had his boys pick the stones and, according to Betty, had the house built in 1914. She said that the back and sides were constructed by "some men he hired, maybe some neighbours," and the evidence would support this memory, as the stones of these three sides are uncut and laid with seeming abandon.

In striking contrast, the stones of the principal façade, which features a bay window

Betty, who married the youngest of the three Stevenson boys, was unclear about some details of her in-laws' early history, but she did know that her husband, John, was born in Edinburgh, Scotland,

and open porch, were precisely squared and laid in the random ashlar style. Each is outlined with a raised joint. The masterly hands of a trained stonemason have never been more evident. Those hands were Charlie Parker's.

"Grampa was very proud of Charlie's work," said Betty.

Like Eddie Parker's house thirty kilometres north at Cardross, which Charlie and Eddie built three years later, the Stevenson house shows evidence of familiarity with an architectural style becoming common in North America at the time. The wide eaves, low-pitched roof with a dormer, and the open porch with tapered piers are suggestive of the Craftsman style, the American version of the Arts and Crafts movement of England.

While linked to a style popularized in magazines of the day, the Stevenson house is unique in its detailing. The living-room fireplace, for example, shows Charlie Parker's distinctively artistic work in its use of colour, style, and craftsmanship, and the concrete steps and floor of the porch are incised with whimsical scrolls carried out with a sure but unknown hand. A shingled porch off the back door, however, was obviously an afterthought: crazily balanced on boulders of assorted sizes, it allegedly was added for Mary's collection of geraniums, her favourite flower.

Robert was no carpenter but he could cut meat, which is why he raised sheep. Today, rolls of rusting page wire near where the barn once stood attest to his sizable flock, and neighbours remember him peddling meat throughout the "South Country."

Betty's memories of life in the stone house dated to 1939, when she arrived to teach at Spring Mount School and boarded with Robert and Mary about a kilometre down the road. After she and John married, they all lived in the stone house till she and John built their own home. Betty was not unhappy to leave the fieldstone house, but not for seemingly obvious reasons: "I never liked the looks of the stone – too barren. The front is a work of art, but the rest is just a stone pile."

The latter may be its fate. Robert and Mary moved into Assiniboia in 1952, Robert

died in 1955, and the land was sold shortly after. It's been empty since the early 1960s.

Alone in a lonely landscape, it still commands a heart-aching view of uninhabited fields rolling away below. On a sweet spring day, the fragrance from the lilacs and the apple trees in the orchard suggests hope. The resident raccoons and the windows of jagged glass suggest otherwise. But perhaps, one day, soon . . . ❧

The difference between the cobblestone and cut-stone application is clearly evident at the southwest corner of the Stevenson house.

The fine craftsmanship evident in the fireplace is a standard trademark of Charlie Parker's interior work.

The Langrish Farmhouse

NEAR OXBOW

William Langrish claimed a homestead "at the end of the earth," says Marie Mahan, and for this she is grateful. ❧ William came from England to what is now southeast Saskatchewan in 1884. He chose land in the Souris Valley because he expected the Manitoba and South Western Railway to arrive nearby within a year or two, and because of the proximity of a coal field in an area of "long cold winters" and scarce firewood. ❧ The beauty of the setting – on the outside curve of an oxbow in the Souris River, which allows views up and down the broad, flat valley – was not recorded as a reason for his decision. But maybe, subconsciously, it was. ❧ In an 1891 letter to his Member of Parliament, Minister of the Interior Edgar Dewdney, William explained that less than half of his homestead and pre-emption

that his pre-emption be granted as a second, $10 homestead registration fee. Although Department of the Interior officials were against the petition, because it defeated the purpose of enticing more settlers out West, Dewdney complied.

William's "sole purpose in coming to this country was to become a bonafide settler," and he sincerely tried to fulfill his obligations: in 1886, he and a friend built a 14-by-16-foot (4 m × 5 m), storey-and-a-half, concrete cottage. Here, amazingly, he and three other bachelors once held a party, making cookies, bread, and sixty pies for the sixty guests who stayed until dawn the next day.

He also worked hard, taking on railway construction in the northern States after spring seeding was completed. And at the age of thirty-three, he was able to marry. He chose eighteen-year-old English-born Nellie Harwood, who'd moved to the area to live with her uncle and aunt while her widowed father, an accountant, travelled with Cornelius Van Horne on Canadian Pacific Railway business.

was "fit for arable land." This, in addition to poor weather and the no-show railway, had prevented him from paying the $3-per-acre pre-emption fee. "Knowing how you always take into consideration the wants and petitions of your constituents," he asked

In later years, William wrote a long account of "Pioneer Days in the Oxbow and Alameda District" – the CPR arrived in 1891, but not where a railway was expected, which caused the first Alameda, located about six kilometres northwest of William's Valley Farm, to move to its present site, and created Oxbow about five kilometres northeast of William's farm – but, unfortunately, never anything about his fieldstone home.

It is known that his two-and-a half-storey house was built by Bob McIlvenna, who had trained as a stonemason in Ontario and became an 1882 homesteader in what became the Oxbow area. McIlvenna's style was plain – the stones, all similar in width, are squared and laid in careful courses; small, sometimes wedged, stones make up the slightly curved lintels – but competent.

The only factual evidence of the home's age is a stamped 1903 picture-postcard of the house. Neither this nor other early but undated photographs show the gracious open veranda now wrapped around two sides. Nothing has been written about the veranda's construction either, but educated guesses date it to about 1920, with Bob McIlvenna's son Bill as the stonemason.

While the interior was simple, with rooms leading off a central hall, the Langrish home was nevertheless considered "the fanciest house in the district," says Nellie Collopy, William and Nellie's niece, who was born in it in 1913. Most impressive was the second-floor bathroom with its flush toilet, the water for it pumped up from the river. Her contemporaries recalled picnics in the "Langrish woods" directly across the river, and photographs show a rudimentary footbridge to these woods.

William and Nellie left this idyllic site in 1925, planning to join their son in Florida but soon returning to retire in Oxbow. Their land and home was rented out until 1946, when Ross and Helen (Deyell) Hames, descendants of the area's first settlers, bought it. Their daughter Marie and her husband, Ken, took over the mixed farming operation in 1978.

Marie still delights in her childhood home, revelling in

the technologies that connect her to the outside world and, equally, in the evidence of ancient history at her doorstep: concretions of shells from when, millions of years ago, the area was covered with a sea; and stone hammerheads possibly from as far back as five thousand years, when First Nations people travelled through and camped in the Souris Valley, itself the result of drainage from glacial Lake Regina.

Although part of an important trade and migration route for First Nations, the Langrish homestead was never on the way to anywhere else for those who came later, however. Some local folk are surprised to hear it exists. And Marie likes it that way.

"Every day I think how beautiful it is. I look around and think it's the best place in the world to live." ✻

An imposing veranda, added in the 1920s, features heavy square columns on a sturdy fieldstone wall.

Gestingthorpe

THE SERJEANT FARMHOUSE, NEAR SUMMERBERRY

Nothing is more romantic than a castle overlooking a lake, especially a castle shrouded in mystery. And so it is with Gestingthorpe, the 1890 fieldstone home of Bernard Serjeant and his wife, Ada. In truth, Gestingthorpe is known as "the castle" only because of its original crenellated tower, now foreshortened due to lightening. Its lake is a wide, deep slough. The Serjeants, however, have always been a mystery. According to his gravestone, Bernard was born in 1861, second son of James Serjeant, vicar of Acton, Suffolk, England. According to *Grit and Growth: The Story of Grenfell* by Annie Yule, he paid $500 to learn farming at Winmarleigh Grange, a Grenfell-area farm with a grand home established in 1883 by Richard Lake, who later became lieutenant-governor of Saskatchewan,

The lean-to summer kitchen was a common feature to keep the heat of cooking out of the rest of the house.

and Lake's father, a military hero. Along with other English settlers in the district, the Lakes attempted to re-create the values of the British gentry. Although they owned land and purebred cattle, they hired others to carry out the work associated with these endeavours, and are locally remembered for their polo playing, horse races, and hunting with hounds.

While the Serjeants are not included in written accounts of these aristocratic pursuits, Bernard not only continued to live as a gentleman farmer after he acquired his own land ten kilometres south of Summerberry, he and Ada also set themselves apart from their neighbours.

Even their home – specifically its square, three-storey tower with battlements – was unique. Its stonemason is unknown, though he could have been one of the Scots from the neighbouring Moffat area.

The purpose of the tower is also a guessing game. According to various stories, it was valued for its view of the stars, the wide perspective it offered on annual regattas on the lake, and for "their blue-blooded friends to watch polo matches on the field south of the lake." It is a fact, however, that the Union Jack was raised from the top of it at the dawn of each and every day.

West of this English-cottage-with-a-tower was a stone barn built into the hill, its loft at ground level. Each stall was graced with a brass plaque naming the resident horse. The son of the subsequent owner says the Serjeants "ranched polo ponies," while a neighbour has written of a small herd of Aberdeen Angus cattle and four Clydesdale horses.

All histories agree on one point: the Serjeants, including John Serjeant, of whom nothing is known except that he died at Gestingthorpe in 1912 at the age of forty-seven, never lifted a hand in the care of their livestock or their half-section of land. They didn't work at all, in fact. Albert Murrell, whose past is unrecorded, was their butler, valet, and hired man, and lived in a small, separate house on the property. Susan Jane Mead, who had emigrated from England with her husband and seven children before her husband abandoned her, worked as a maid and slept in the tower where, according to a descendant, mice ran over the bed she shared with a daughter.

The Serjeants attended St. Andrew's Anglican Church about sixteen kilometres east of their home, and it was in the adjacent cemetery that Ada was buried after her death in February 1914. The epitaph on her headstone adds to the intrigue. "But pray ye that your flight be not in winter" is thought to be a comment on the difficulties of burial in winter, but because the couple always "kept to themselves" and Bernard obviously saw no reason to change after his wife died, nobody is certain. Engraved on her footstone is an eighteenth-century Latin poem in praise of God, followed by "Gestingthorpe 1792." The significance of the latter is unknown.

Bernard followed Ada to the grave in 1921. He willed his estate to two brothers: Edward, who soon arrived

to live in the house, and Farel, who was an English professor at McGill University, Montreal, and came out after he retired. They are remembered for their chauffeured drive to St. Andrew's every Sunday: they would sit in their "big black car" until entering a back pew at the end of the first hymn, leaving their man to wait in the car.

The Serjeant brothers lived at Gestingthorpe until selling it in 1945 and moving into Wolseley. After Edward died in 1947, Farel moved to Victoria, British Columbia, where he died in 1956.

Albert Murrell also moved to British Columbia, alone and with plans to write a book about life with the Sergeants. But his account has disappeared, so the dream that became Gestingthorpe remains unrecorded. And, although its tower is still picturesque above the quiet water, a widening crack climbs it from one window to the next. Caraganas crowd the empty bay window, while Manitoba maples threaten to engulf the whole. Only another dream will rescue Gestingthorpe. ❧

Even in its ruined state, the massing of the Serjeant house evokes a sense of awe in visitors.

The Bird Farmhouse

NEAR WHITEWOOD

The Bird home had it all: good looks and personality. It's as rare in a house as it is in a person. ❧ Built in 1892–93 at what became known as Bird's Point on Round Lake in the Qu'Appelle Valley, its history goes back to Viscount Charles de Cazes. The second son of Count de Cazes of France, Charles was known in western Canada as "the Count." Born in 1839, Charles allegedly sailed to Quebec with his father and siblings in the 1860s to escape renewed revolutionary rumblings. He moved to Winnipeg in the 1870s and married widow Margaret Griffin, daughter of Chief Factor James Bird (whose land grant is now Bird's Hill Provincial Park in Manitoba) of the Hudson's Bay Company. ❧ In 1883, Charles filed for a homestead on a Round Lake peninsula sixteen kilometres north of Whitewood. Because he met

The mansard roof lines extend from the main structure onto the back addition, and both units display dormer windows.

the homesteading requirements, including the construction of a frame house for his wife and three children, his application for his patent and pre-emption was approved in February 1890. A month later, his patent and pre-emption were deeded to Robert Machray and Duncan MacArthur.

Duncan MacArthur was a Winnipeg banker, and Robert Machray was the Anglican archbishop of the Ecclesiastical Province of Rupert's Land. Both were executors and trustees of the Dr. Curtis Bird estate. Dr. Curtis Bird was Margaret de Cazes's

brother, the youngest of the fifteen children born to Factor Bird and his several wives. Dr. Bird had died in 1876, two years after his second wife. A letter written by Dr. Bird's granddaughter, Betty Bird Pidcock, states that Dr. Bird's 1876 will left his estate to the two young sons of his second marriage, George (Jack) and Colin Bird. Robert Machray was appointed guardian of these boys, ages six and four at the time.

Although Betty did not explain why the land belonging to her grandfather's sister and brother-in-law was included in her grandfather's

estate, she subsequently wrote about the boys' visits with their Uncle and Aunt de Cazes, and their tales of picking saskatoons for winemaking and being chastised, in French, for their manners.

The book *More Edmonton Stories* by Tony Cashman continues the de Cazes story. Apparently, after leaving his homestead, Charles became an Indian agent in Edmonton and, in the 1890s, began building a fieldstone "castle" on what was later called Castle Island in Lac Ste. Anne, Alberta.

The two young Bird boys, meanwhile, boarded at St. John's College School in Winnipeg and, when Jack turned twenty-one in 1891, the Round Lake land was transferred to him. When Colin, Betty's father, turned twenty-one two years later, he bought the land from Jack, who then left for the United States.

Betty Bird Pidcock wrote little about the fieldstone house on what she called "the ranch," except that it was built by her father, Colin, and its stonemason was Eric Berg. Eric, who learned his trade in Sweden and immigrated with his wife and a child to the New Stockholm District in 1887, is also responsible for St. Mary the Virgin Anglican Church in Whitewood. Other than the random rubble style, however, there is nothing to suggest Eric's hand in both buildings. Unlike the church, the arches over the Bird windows are of two rows of bricks laid with their ends outward, and yellow brick is used for quoining every window, door, and corner.

Evidence of the way Eric and other early stonemasons split large stones remains in the sides of two matched grey stones in the Bird house: in each is one-half of two round holes drilled into the stone. Originally, the intact holes had been filled with water and capped. During the following winter, the water expanded and split the rock apart.

Although the top of the home's mansard roof is now slightly pitched to aid drainage, the exterior is generally in its original state. The interior is not. The ceiling has been stripped of its plaster ornamentation, most of the woodwork is gone, and the open staircase to the second floor has been enclosed. The fireplace is now a niche near the floor of a room that was once two, and the billiard room with its separate entrance to the outside is a bedroom.

Although the fieldstone milkhouse remains intact beside the spring-fed creek behind the house, the grounds have also changed. Betty Bird Pidcock said there was once a track for horse races south of the house, but it is now a grainfield, and the fieldstone barn is only a huge hole filled with the remains of its walls.

The Birds are long gone too. Colin married a Wapella girl in 1903, "the money in the Bird estate ran out," and the stone house was sold in 1905.

A Swedish couple ensured the continuation of the Bird holdings. Per and Johanna

Stendahl bought the land in 1921, raised their nine children in the stone house, farmed and also operated a resort that had sprung up along the shores of Bird's Point. One of the Stendahls' sons lived in the stone house till he died in 2001. Aging gracefully – which is also rare – the home is still in the family. ৯

A stone milkhouse stands nearby, a permanent reminder of an earlier era when dairy products were kept cold with ice blocks in such structures.

The symmetrical details of the Bird farmhouse create a pleasing blend of stone, brick, wood, and glass.

OPPOSITE: Although the front entrance to the building was significantly modified in the 1950s, the overall design of the Turton farmhouse retains the historic flavour that defined the house during its initial construction in 1890.

Rosemount

THE TURTON FARMHOUSE, NEAR CANNINGTON MANOR

A yellowing photograph of a fieldstone house is glued to the cover of Madge McCullough's scrapbook. Below it is the location – fifteen miles (24 km) north of Manor – and the words "Rich in history, valuable in memory." Characteristically, however, Madge left it up to others – clippings from the North American press – to reveal the darkest side of this history and memory. ❧ The scrapbook begins with John Turton, who left England for Ontario in 1869 and later travelled to Manitoba. Here he met and married English-born Priscilla Adelaide Arniel. They arrived in Moose Mountain in the spring of 1882. ❧ "He thought it was a grand trip. Mother would never even talk about it. It wasn't any picnic for her with two babies and a third under the apron," wrote their seventh child. They

An early photo of the Turton farmhouse as originally designed and built in 1890. (Corrie Hart)

eventually had seventeen, but only twelve lived long enough to be named.

In 1890, the Turtons replaced their log home with Rosemount, a two-storey field-stone home built by Ontario-trained stonemason William G. Anderson of Arcola. Cruci-form in shape, with a frame cupola enclosing a bell, the

The west side of the Turton farmhouse includes a substantial enclosed porch, also added in the 1950s.

front projection featured a pointed-arch window under the gable roof and a door on each side. All the stones were large, cut and laid in a coursed style. All the corners, windows, and doors had lime-stone quoins, and all the doors and windows limestone lintels.

Although they built a house that rivalled those of the English gentry at nearby Can-nington Manor, and they took part in the Cannington races, fairs, dances, and church activities, the Turtons were no dilettantes. They were among those who organized the first district school – Glen Ade-laide, after Mrs. Turton – and they farmed most of the land in the district. They were also known for their hospitality:

the back part of the second floor was named "Bummer's Roost" for all the travellers who were given a bed there.

But it is the Turton tragedy that once seized the attention of readers as far away as New York and is still the topic of articles in newspapers and magazines. What happened, however, and what was report-ed were two – or a dozen – different things.

The one known fact is that three-year-old Gertie Turton disappeared from home in August 1893 and, despite a massive search by neighbours and members of the White Bear Reserve, was never found. Adelaide was convinced Gertie was taken by "the Indians." This is when the newspapers picked up the story, exaggerat-ing it to the point of including a silver mug that identified her and, at the last minute, pre-vented her marriage to a Sioux brave called Black Dog.

The Turtons finally did find a Gertie. Although it was proven that a fifteen-year-old South Dakota girl, daughter of a Sioux woman and a white man, was not the lost Gertie, the Turtons adopted her in 1898 and renamed her Gertrude.

Adelaide died in 1920, when their horse-drawn vehicle overturned and John was unable to lift it from on top of her. By the time he got back with help, she was dead. He died three years later, and the subsequent family squabbles resulted in the loss of the house.

By 1937, the house had been empty for a number of years. Sparrows and gophers had taken up residence, and under the collapsed barn were two dead horses. But, although Madge McCullough later confessed that she cried when they bought the stone house, the lush green of the Moose Mountain area was better than the drought-stricken Ponteix farm she and her husband, Ed, had left.

The McCulloughs immediately began increasing their family to three plus a foster child. They established a purebred Hereford operation, raised certified seed, and named their farm Bonnie-mede. They became involved in the new Co-operative Commonwealth Federation and, in the 1945 federal election, Ed was elected as a CCF Member of Parliament for Assiniboia. He subsequently lost, won twice, and lost for the last time in 1958.

Major renovations to the house began in 1950. Madge's father, Samuel Rogers, owned a sawmill, so all the new woodwork was made by him from Moose Mountain birch. This included a front door with side lights, a new staircase in the centre hall, and all new nine-pane windows.

Charlie Parker, the Kennedy stonemason responsible for the chalet at Moose Mountain Provincial Park, undertook the changes to the exterior: the front projection was reduced to become a covered entrance with a wide arch and two windows under a new hipped roof. "1890" was carved in the keystone.

An uncut-stone porch was also built over the outside entrance to the cellar, and open and closed porches were added to the west side. A cobblestone finish was later added to the closed porch, but neither it nor the cellar porch suggests Charlie's finesse.

By the time the renovations were complete, Ed was on to something else. Eventually he created a resort and had a large log home built on nearby Cannington Lake. Ed and Madge died in the 1990s and their son Jerry moved into the stone house in 1998, but he died in it in 2001.

By 2005, Jerry's daughter, Corrie Hart, and her husband had given up their British Columbia holdings for Bonniemede. She said she had no choice: "My grandmother wanted to keep the house in the family. It's an honour and a privilege to live here." ⁊

A rejuvenated Turton farmhouse stands majestically amidst the Moose Mountain hills of southeastern Saskatchewan.

The Lolacher Farmhouse

NEAR ZEHNER

Little wonder that Jacob Lolacher and many of his homesteading neighbours chose to build their homes with stone. It was almost preordained. ❧ About 12,000 years prior to Jacob's arrival in the Zehner district, the last continental ice sheet to cover what is now Saskatchewan stalled on its way back to the north. Its retreating margin, transversing the province in a northwesterly direction, crossed through the Zehner/Pilot Butte area. ❧ During its original advance, this glacier had eroded areas to the north, including the Canadian Shield north of Creighton, and carried with it an unsorted mix of gravel, sand, silt, and clay, with boulders scattered throughout like raisins in a cake. Melting in place during the stagnant stage of its retreat, this mix was dropped, covering the Zehner district as well as a broad section

The Lolacher farmhouse
is an excellent example of the harmony
that can be achieved when you integrate
good design and construction with
well-planned landscaping.

of land that stretches as far north as the Qu'Appelle Valley.

Because the flow of water was relatively fast at the melting margin of the stagnant glacier, smaller stones such as gravel, sand, and silt were deposited and formed the eastern shore of glacial Lake Regina. Today's Pilot Butte is located on this former shoreline, while the Regina plain is the old lake bottom, composed of the layers of silt and clay that eventually settled out of the glacial meltwater.

Jacob didn't care about the reasons for the stones on his 160 acres of land, but he did recognize their potential as building material. In 1898, three years after he arrived and applied for the patent to this land, the largest of his fieldstones formed the walls of the home he built on and into a knoll.

Family records include the Department of the Interior documents granting Jacob his homestead in the District of Assiniboia, North-West Territories, in 1899, but little else. Descendants know only that Jacob and his wife, Caroline, came from Germany.

German stonemason John Zinkhan, however, was Jacob's friend, and John's granddaughter, Anita Ring, says that her grandfather and another German stonemason, Ed Fuchs, helped Jacob build his home. These three men also built the nearby Arrat Roman Catholic Church. South of Jacob's land, Jacob and John built the much smaller Leibel home, which also emerges from a berm. When John built his own fieldstone home on the stone-free Regina plain, formerly glacial Lake Regina, in 1905, he had no material, so he had oxen haul stones from Jacob's land.

Jacob and John built to last. Although differing in architectural and stonemasonry styles, both their homes are still straight and solid. The segmental brick arches over Jacob's doors and windows remain tightly intact, and his walls of random rubble construction have needed only the occasional repointing.

Inside Jacob Lolacher's home, however, only the windowsills – 65 centimetres deep on the bottom level and 50 centimetres on the top – suggest the original appearance. Jacob's granddaughter Annie Chervinski recalls, "You could sit on a windowsill as easily as sitting on a chair," but even they took on a new look after the Lolacher family sold their home in 1975. The buyer gutted the house from top to bottom, insulated, and refinished the interior to sell as a modern three-storey walkout.

"The difference between then and now is like night and day," says Annie.

When Annie and her two siblings were growing up, for example, they lived in the lowest level, which contained a kitchen, living room, bedroom and, because there was no basement, a walk-in cold-cellar. In the summer, they slept on the second level, which opened directly onto the yard. The third floor was so cold they hung meat in it during the winter and, in the summer, kept "chickens sitting for clucks."

While her stories include the horrors of the Depression and tales of picking pails full of small stones in a Sisyphean effort to clear the fields, Annie also tells of rollicking days and nights: "Oh the parties we had! Every birthday and anniversary. We'd be baking for days: cabbage rolls, buns, strudel, chocolates by the gallon. Homemade sausage. Dill pickles from the big barrel behind the door. All the German dances were held at our house, on the second floor. Lots of wine and homebrew . . ."

Their homebrew activities were never discovered, she adds. "We were lucky." Or maybe it was the elevated location and total lack of trees, ensuring a clear view of the roads for kilometres around. The thousands of trees and shrubs that now frame the house are relatively recent, planted in 1983 by a couple who, like three generations of Lolachers, raised their family within the stone walls. They still visit the home.

And the affection continues. Kathryn Drope, who bought the Lolacher home in 1999 with her husband, Michael, says, "There are times when I drive in this yard and say, 'Thank you Jacob.'" ❧

The low placement of the doorway suggests that a veranda, common to turn of the twentieth-century homes, was not envisioned for this farmhouse.

CENTRE LEFT: The segmented arches over the windows are executed in a buff brick.

Urban Homes

Fieldstone homes in Saskatchewan's urban settings are remembered because they are rare. But, whether grand or humble, the same cannot always be said about their original owners. Often pillars of a community that has no memory of them, they include the surgeon who "brought his work home," entrepreneurs with a rakish eye and a fedora at a jaunty angle, and lovers whose shipboard romance continued on the Canadian plain then ended tragically. The staid streets of Saskatchewan cities, towns, and villages are not what they might appear.

Saskatchewan's earliest urban communities evolved out of fur trade and mission posts along the Saskatchewan River. Cumberland House dates back to 1774. Towns such as Prince Albert (1866) boasted many fine private residences well before the railway cut through the open prairie of present-day southern Saskatchewan in the 1880s. However, it is at these latter locations that most of the late nineteenth-century construction booms took place. ❧ Many early prairie towns and villages were quite accurately referred to as "tent cities": the lack of adequate building materials resulted in families and even businesses being accommodated in tents, some featuring false fronts, until the necessary building supplies could be transported by rail. ❧ Residential buildings tended to be of frame construction.

ABOVE: Regina – a tent and false-fronted town in the early 1880s. (Saskatchewan Archives Board R-A 8700)

The stone manse erected in 1894 and St. Peter's Anglican Church, Qu'Appelle, share a common white picket fence. A relatively new tree already begins to hide the manse from public view. (Saskatchewan Archives Board R-B 3581)

However, as individuals prospered and communities grew, masonry houses started to appear. These were often second-generation structures, replacing inferior temporary earlier buildings. Where settlers had sufficient means to build well, their homes were built of brick or stone at the outset. Some of those stone houses have survived fires, wind storms, and urban renewal, and stand today as some of Saskatchewan's finest historic residences. Those built before 1900 often have distinctive architectural influences, sometimes reflecting the areas from whence the pioneers came. These features include mansard roofs, bay windows, and decorative bargeboard in gable ends. As the twentieth century progressed, such features became less prominent, or disappeared altogether.

Urban residences made of stone were generally either one or two storey, the former often sporting a cottage or hip roof; while storey-and-a-half and two-storey houses were more often found with gable end roofs or variations of the hip roof.

Cobblestones – smaller fieldstones – became a popular building material in the 1920s and 1930s, particularly for recreational structures in Canada's national parks but also for stone residences. These smaller unsplit stones enabled some stonemasons to apply only a veneer of stone to a frame house, rather than building the entire bearing walls of stone.

In a town setting, the more ornate homes were often situated on corner lots, where the impressiveness of their design could be more fully appreciated. In a few instances, the more grandiose homes actually occupy a full city block, with extensive complementary landscaping.

At first, as with any new home, the lack of a mature surrounding landscape often made the building design seem very stark. Later, as trees, hedges, flower gardens, and fences were introduced, urban homes took on a pastoral appearance, but if overdone, these enhancements would effectively hide the natural beauty and warmth of the colourful stones.

During the twentieth century, many fine stone houses were inappropriately renovated. Often the original multi-paned windows were replaced with single-pane sealed units. Options for retaining and improving existing storm windows were generally deemed too costly. Likewise, many original cedar shingle roofs have been replaced with asphalt or sheet metal. As a result, few historic stone houses today still display their full attractive historic character. However, as owners of heritage homes become more aware of the historic value of original building materials, an increasing number of quality restorations are occurring throughout the province. These owners see themselves, not as temporary occupants, but as stewards in a continuing line of people to occupy their historic house.

In this historic photo, the Edwards house in Broadview, with its decorative bargeboard along the roofline, remains fairly prominent in the community. While mature trees are not yet visible, a newly planted hedge begins to encroach on the property. (Broadview Historical Museum Association)

Rossdhu

THE COLQUHOUN HOUSE, BROADVIEW

The Rossdhu Castle keep is all that remains of the original Clan Colquhoun seat on a Loch Lomond peninsula in Scotland. The castle's other stones were used to build a mansion for the chiefs of Clan Colquhoun in the eighteenth century. It too was called Rossdhu, Gaelic for "dark headland." ❧ This was the family history that accompanied Adam, Mary, and John Colquhoun when they left their home near Dumbarton, Scotland, in 1893, and the reason they called their Broadview home Rossdhu. A comparison of the two buildings suggests it was a pretentious choice, but a comparison of their respective histories – Rossdhu in Scotland is now a golf course clubhouse – suggests that it is finally fitting. ❧ Adam was forty-eight when he, his wife, and their thirty-year-old son arrived in Canada to settle at

ABOVE: An elaborate chimney design again incorporates the brick quoins seen at the corners and surrounding the doors and windows.

RIGHT: The Colquhoun house early in the twentieth century, with a picket fence. The decorative bargeboard in the gables – a common architectural feature on late nineteenth-century homes – is noticeably absent. (Broadview Historical Museum Association)

Donald, British Columbia, a Canadian Pacific Railway divisional point. Adam became a CPR storeskeeper and John a mechanic.

Four years later, Adam quit his job because, as a Presbyterian, he refused to work on Sunday. Leaving Mary and John in Donald, he moved to Broadview, a CPR divisional point as well and, with its central location, one he believed had a promising future.

Mary and John joined Adam in Broadview in 1898. Adam had allegedly built a frame store with living quarters above, and John became the store's trader, hauling merchandise out to the Indian reserves around the nearby

Qu'Appelle Valley to barter for furs. Homesteaders bartered for merchandise with their butter, eggs, and grain.

The Colquhouns prospered. Not only did they allegedly build Broadview's first elevator to handle all their bartered grain, they also built a large, two-storey brick store. It was widely admired for its hardwood floors, plate-glass showcases, embossed metal ceiling, overhead cash-carriers and an inventory that varied from harnesses and hardware to groceries, clothing, and furniture.

In 1907, the same year the store opened, Adam became the first mayor of the newly incorporated town of Broadview.

Life was good. By that time, Adam and Mary had already spent two years in their new home, a two-storey fieldstone house of many gables and several bays, all of which had windows of varying sizes and shapes to allow sunlight to brighten every room. The random-rubble style of the stonemasonry was framed with brick quoins, with most of the gently arched windows quoined as well. The brickwork showed to particular advantage in the impressive exterior chimneys and the two round-headed windows under sharply angled gables in the roof line over the porch.

This porch, its flat roof originally outlined with a balustrade and accessed through one of the round-headed windows, is interesting for its use of bricks of two different colours: most are grey, but some are the same buff colour as those making up the quoins. The Broadview brick factory, in which Adam and his son had invested, made buff-coloured bricks, which would account for their generous use in this house, but, as with the Wolseley Town Hall

and Opera House, the local factory may not have been able to supply all the material, causing the use of a second, different-coloured product.

The inclusion of local brick, however, is speculation only. Nothing about the origins of this house is known for sure. The suggested date of construction ranges from 1890 to 1905, and two stone-masons have been suggested as its builder. No records of the interior are available either, and today's appearance – notably fir woodwork and art glass in the transoms – tells nothing, as a 1928 fire caused extensive damage and a subsequent owner removed the two fireplaces. Adding to the many mysteries is the undocumented story of a portable police cell in a room with its own entrance.

The decline of the family fortunes, however, is well known. Adam, ordered by his doctor to improve his health with a trip to Scotland, died there in 1909. Mary remained in the house until she died about 1929. Finances, meanwhile, staggered under the bankruptcy of the brick factory, and the destruction of the grain elevator and the brick store by fire. The 1929 stock market crash, along with the Dirty Thirties, finished off all Colquhoun business interests in 1933.

Still, there was a time . . .

As a Broadview-area woman, Edna Elder, once wrote about her childhood visits to the Colquhoun store: "'Mr. Colquhoun would insist that his wife would be dreadfully offended if we 'didna' call and see her. She lived in a beautiful stone house surrounded by large trees. She was small and looked a bit like Queen Victoria. The accent and regal surroundings made me think this was Dumbarton Castle. If it had been, I am sure I could not have been more awed.'" ❧

Labourers work on the Colquhoun house to repair the damage caused by a fire in 1928. (Saskatchewan Archives Board R-A 18,787)

OPPOSITE: Situated right across from the town's most prominent landmark, the 1906 Town Hall–Opera House, the Magee house pre-dated it by several years.

The Magee House

WOLSELEY

A ccording to the 1913 *History of the Province of Saskatchewan,* Wolseley was incorporated as a town in 1898, and Robert Armstrong Magee "was given the distinction of first choice for the office of Mayor, serving for two successive terms." One hundred years later, however, neither the name nor the distinction was remembered. ❧ But then, in 2000, Robert Armstrong Magee's home was designated a municipal heritage property, and the restoration of both the building and the name began. ❧ "R.A.," as he was known, was born of Irish descent near the Gatineau River, Quebec. In 1883, at the age of nineteen, he followed his older brother to Grenfell, and two years later moved to Wolseley. He joined the Moose Mountain Scouts that same summer, and was honoured with a medal for

The flared mansard roof on the Magee house is a classic example of a Second Empire–style building. Brick quoins highlight the corners, as well as the door and windows, which are also topped with segmented brick arches.

Was the mansard roof, a feature characteristic of the architectural style known as Second Empire and named for the reign of Napoleon III, chosen for its reflection of R.A.'s home province? Or, as has also been suggested, was it chosen because it provides more living space on the second floor than other roof designs?

Curiosity about the person responsible for the home's design is also piqued by the dormer windows, which drop into the walls instead of remaining within the steep slope of the roof, as in most mansard roofs. The modified mansard roof on the bay and brick addition are other thoughtful details.

The bricks used as quoining material at all corners, including the doors and windows, raise questions as well. Were they, like many of those used to build the Wolseley Town Hall and Opera House across the street, from R.A.'s own factory?

A few facts are known, however. According to Bill McCall of Indian Head, the house was built by his grandfather, William McCall, and

his patrol of the international boundary on horseback during the North-West Rebellion.

R.A., his brother Richard, and a local businessman subsequently formed Magee and Thompson Co., general merchants dealing in everything from groceries to lumber and coal. The company also operated a grist mill, livery barn, and brickyard, and records show that the contractors for the 1894–95 Territorial Courthouse in Wolseley, now a provincial heritage site, were

R.A. and E.A. Banbury, co-founder of Beaver Lumber.

In a ceremony conducted by the bride's father, a Presbyterian minister, R.A. married Eleanor Campbell in 1891. Their one child, a son, died of typhoid fever at the age of seven. The anguish that accompanied this tragedy was cloaked by the walls of the home R.A. and Eleanor had built in 1896.

Little is known about the original design of this 1,336-square-foot (124 m2) home.

John Hutson, Scottish stonemasons who home-steaded in the Moffat area south of Wolseley.

As well, although the parlour's brick bay is not shown in the 1905 Fire Underwriter's Survey, it was part of the original construction, says James Taylor, who bought the house in 2000 and, when stripping the interior lathe and plaster, exposed substantial beams inset into the stone walls to support the bay on each side.

The Underwriter's Survey does show a small wooden structure attached to the back of the house, and James says the late Annie Edwards, who arrived in Wolseley as a three-year-old in 1913, remembered this as a summer kitchen. She told him that the present brick addition

replacing it was completed in 1920.

In that year, R.A. was still serving his second term as a Liberal Member of the Legislative Assembly representing the Moose Mountain constituency. During that time, states his 1957 obituary in the *Leader-Post,* "He spoke to the address from the throne on the subject of the extension of franchise to women and also on the subject of 'banishing the bar.'" His pro-temperance stand was well known locally as well. R.A. became sheriff and local registrar for the Judicial District of Moosomin in 1922, an appointment that dictated his subsequent residency in Moosomin. He retired, eventually to British Columbia, in 1939.

His Wolseley home, how-

ever, is still serving the public good: Scientists with the Saskatchewan Research Council and Canada Mortgage and Housing Corporation installed sensors in the walls to monitor the temperature and moisture content of the structural wood beams imbedded in the stone walls. The results will offer new information about the effect of adding insulation to the inside of a stone wall on the structural wood members, a particular concern when stone buildings of heritage value are being restored. 🦢

ABOVE: The brick quoins form a pleasing contrast to the cut stones making up the basic structure of the walls.

FAR LEFT: The dormer windows that extend from the roof into the stone walls are key elements of this late-nineteenth-century house.

Bushey Park House

THE BUSHE RESIDENCE, GRENFELL

It was a fairytale romance that began aboard a ship bound for South Africa, continued in India and England, and ended in a stone house in Grenfell, North-West Territories, Canada. ❧ Dr. Cecil Josiah Lambton Bushe was born of a prominent Irish family. According to his great grandson, he was the grandson of Sir Charles Kendal Bushe, Chief Justice of Ireland, and the son of Seymour Bushe, crown prosecutor in Dublin. As Seymour's second son, he followed the British tradition of joining the army. Before receiving the royal commission that resulted in his position as surgeon major in the British Imperial Army, however, he studied medicine at Dublin University. ❧ Meanwhile, Ailleen Mary Beatrice Hosmer was born of an Anglican bishop and his wife on the island of Madeira off Portugal,

The Bushe residence is set well back from the road, permitting a variety of landscape options to the owners over the years.

grew up with servants in Somerset, England, and summered in the south of France.

While sailing to South Africa with her parents, Ailleen met Cecil, who was on his way to take part in the Zulu War. They married in Capetown in 1880.

Ten years and five children later, having served in India and England, Cecil retired, took his full pension, and, having been impressed with Canada during a previous trip to its eastern parts, acquired 960 acres about fifteen kilo-

metres southeast of Grenfell. He had a fine home built overlooking a small lake and named it Kilfane after his cousin's similar home in Ireland.

Among Kilfane's various farm buildings were a stone barn for the cattle, a wooden barn for the horses and hunting hounds, and a bunkhouse for the farm workers, all of which were necessary for a gentleman farmer. There was a British-born governess for the children and, among the various diversions, fox hunts

with well-heeled English neighbours.

The youngest Bushe son was born at Kilfane in 1891, the same year the oldest son died.

In 1895, the Bushes moved into Grenfell. Local history suggests that their fieldstone house was built by Richard Talmay, the English-born stonemason responsible for Grenfell's fieldstone school and many of the town's commercial buildings. Like most of these structures, the dressed stone of the Bushe home was highlighted by brick quoining of the windows as well as the walls. All the windows are arched, although in a semi-elliptical curve rather than with a round arch and keystone as in the other Talmay-built structures.

The unusually high number of stone buildings in Grenfell may be explained by a booster section in the October 15, 1898 *Toronto Saturday Globe*. Extolling the virtues of the "beautiful park-like country dotted with pretty poplar bluffs," one writer went on to discuss "the marks of a 'hoary antiquity'" in the many coloured granites and other stones of which its principal buildings are now constructed . . ."

Bushey Park House, as the stone home was called, allowed Cecil to establish a medical practice in town, which helped pay the bills that, judging by the mortgages he took out on the farm, were mounting. He was also involved in a Grenfell beverage factory that sold such treats as sarsaparilla, ginger beer, and champagne cider, and he continued to raise horses on the farm he rented out. Ailleen was president of the Grenfell Hospital Guild she helped to organize.

But the fairytale was drawing to a close. During a trip to Ireland in June 1898, one of the couple's daughters died. Two months later, the youngest daughter was born, but in October that same year, Cecil contracted pneumonia and died. His death occurred thirteen days after the *Toronto Saturday Globe* carried his description of the Grenfell area: "For healthfulness the climate is unsurpassed. Bronchitis and pneumonia are practically unknown. . . ."

Lloyd Arthur, whose family has owned Kilfane since

1934 and who has researched the Bushe family extensively, writes that Ailleen was left "with six children and considerable real estate, but little or no income." By 1901, Bushey Park House was a "first-class" boardinghouse, Ailleen was living in smaller quarters, and another son had died as the result of a hunting accident. She eventually moved to Winnipeg so the remaining boys could go to university. The farm was sold in 1912, and the house in 1917. Ailleen died in 1946 and was buried beside Cecil in the St. Andrew's Anglican Church cemetery, two kilometres south of Kilfane.

Yet another romance involving Bushey Park House began in 1995, however, when Alvin Gallinger saw the fieldstone home on its spacious lot. "I fell in love," he says in explanation of the passion that fueled renovations such as removal of the maid's staircase to create a more functional kitchen, re-creation of the stairs to the central cellar, and enclosure of the two-storey open porch added sometime in the 1920s. He and his wife, Eva, have also returned the interior to an approximation of its appearance in the twenties, and surrounded the house with grounds that have never looked so fine.

"It has lived up to all my hopes," says Alvin simply.

MIDDLE LEFT: The front entry has been set into the south side of the central bay, giving greater privacy and shelter from the prevailing northwest winds.

A group of nine young people enjoy a ride on the new automobile next to the Bushe Residence early in the 20th century. (Grenfell Museum)

The Carpenter Cottage

WAPELLA

This fieldstone cottage on the outskirts of Wapella was once called Jollity Farm, the name of a 1960s British song by the Bonzo Dog Doo Dah Band. Today, the two sane lines in this otherwise Monty-Pythonesque composition are still perfectly descriptive: "Believe me, folks, it's great/For everything sings out to us as we go through the gate." At the time of its naming – 1983 – Jollity Farm was overdue for fun. Even its history had been neglected. Unlike the house, this history still needs attention. A title search reveals its 1897 land owners as: Richard Angus of Montreal; Right Honourable Lord Strathcona (Sir Donald A. Smith) of London, England; Edmund Osler of Toronto; and William Scarth of Ottawa. These men were trustees of the Canada North-West Land Company, which had been incorporated for

A large A-frame gable window extends over the offset front entry.

the purpose of advertising and selling portions of the Canadian Pacific Railway Company's lands in the North-West Territories, and all the CPR's town and village sites to be laid out along the main line between Brandon and the eastern boundary of British Columbia.

In 1901, the land on which the fieldstone cottage was built was sold to Wapella farmer Henry William Carpenter. The 1901 Canada census reveals that Henry

William Carpenter and his wife, Mary, had arrived in Canada from England in 1882 and were residents of Wapella in the year of the census. "H. Wm. Carpenter" is also the name on an exciting find in the attic during the home's 1980s renovation: stacks of a 1890s Chicago newspaper *Farm, Field and Stockman: Agriculture, Gardening and Home Literature.*

The emerging picture of the home's origin is muddied by homestead records, however.

They show that Henry William, born in 1839, built a house on his first homestead northeast of Wapella in 1884, and a house on his second homestead west of Wapella in 1890. He obtained title to the latter in 1904, and, for a period during this activity, he was "living on the outskirts of the village." Three houses built by a homesteader – not a lad at the time – within seventeen years?

The name of the alleged stonemason, Alex Sutherland, is not etched in stone either, as it is based on the word of an elderly Wapella man and tales told to Alex's great-nephew. Scottish-born Alex Sutherland, of Tantallon in the Qu'Appelle Valley north of Wapella, is credited with building barns and at least one house in the valley. His construction of a large, two-storey farmhouse near Wapella has been documented. Still, although the stonework, roofline, and off-centre door of the farmhouse and the Carpenter cottage are similar, the farmhouse lacked the cottage's brick quoins and lintels, a feature favoured by stonemason Richard Talmay, who also farmed near Rocanville northeast of Wapella.

Perhaps the history of this cottage is so vague because it quickly passed from one owner to the next. By the time Dixon and Doreen Cottingham of Moosomin received its title in 1983, it had been uninhabited for several decades. "It was home only to many birds and mice," recalls the Cottinghams' daughter, Kilby, for whom the house had been bought. "There were no intact windows, insulation or plumbing. The floors had rotted and buckled. The stonework had not been maintained. Miraculously, the shake roof was intact and needed very little repair. Likewise, the staircase to the second floor and some of the interior doors."

The three Cottinghams removed the rotted wooden porches collapsing around the front and back doors, and stripped the interior back to the stone and to the earth below the floor joists. There was no foundation, so Dixon removed 1,800 wheelbarrow-loads of dirt to create a concrete-lined cellar for a furnace, staircase, and water tanks. The ceilings were lowered to accommodate heating ducts, and twelve-pane windows were custom-made to fit the eleven windows. Interior walls were reconstructed in their original location, and a main-floor bedroom became a bathroom. Period flooring, mouldings, hardware, doors and cabinets were found, refinished and installed.

"I have lived all over the world and have no reservation about saying that Jollity Farm was one of my very favourite places on the globe. The skies, the air, the storms, the wildlife, the simplicity of it – I was in love with living there. I would be living there happily today, were it not for shortage of work," wrote Kilby in 2006.

When she left, the cottage was sold to a woman who operated it as a teahouse. It returned to private use in 2002, when another woman bought it as a retreat for herself and her husband. First smitten during a trip to visit a friend, she'd taken immediate action when she saw a for-sale sign being posted. "I grew up on a farm in Dorset with walls like this, a sweet little house," she explains. "The

simplicity. And the light is so nice. The bird life. I love it."

Her husband, a retired architect, contributes his professional opinion. "Very Ontario, Ontario as settled by the English: symmetrical with a gable over the front entrance, which had to be off-centre because the house is too small for a central front hall, so the builder had to choose a room on one side or the other in which to place the door. The interior is a similar expression of the exterior: very simple. It has a lot of appeal."

Or, as the Bonzo Dog Doo Dah Band would have it: ". . . everything sings out to us as we go through the gate." ❧

Brick quoins and a segmented arch frame the window in the Carpenter cottage. The authentic wooden windows enhance the historic appearance of this dwelling.

The Smithers House

MOOSOMIN

In October 1892, the *Moosomin Courier* was pleased to reprint a *Manitoba Free Press* story describing Moosomin as "more of a society town than most other places in Manitoba or the North West Territories . . . with two excellent hunt clubs." A subsequent news item mentioned the polo club, noting Lord Tennyson's nephew as a member. ❧ This emphasis on horses as status symbol, as well as the obvious importance of horses as the main form of transportation and farm power, suggests that the owner of the Moosomin Saddlery & Harness Emporium, John Smithers, was well placed for success. ❧ As reported in the December 1896 *Moosomin Spectator,* he achieved that success: "Mr. Smithers came from St. Mary's Ont., landed in Winnipeg in '82, stayed there for some six months and eventually decided to try his

A side view of the house displays a bay window as well as one of the gabled wings of the house. The brick corner quoins are placed at alternating heights from one wall to the next.

lands in the North-West Territories.

The certificate of title suggests that Mary Hannah was the first to own what had been CPR land. But the Town of Moosomin lists the construction date for the Smitherses' fieldstone home as 1889, eight years before the land was purchased.

More questions arise with the assertions by respected local historian Phyllis Henry that the house was built by stonemason George Dalgleish with fieldstones from the Pipestone Valley eight kilometres south and bricks from the Moosomin brick factory. But there is no record of George Dalgleish in Moosomin or its environs, and an academic paper on Saskatchewan's brick factories states that the Moosomin brick factory operated from about 1890 to about 1904.

Phyllis Henry, however, does have an intimate knowledge of the Smithers house. Her parents, Kenneth and Helen Price, bought the house and property from Smithers in 1920, when she was twelve. Because the Smitherses had outlined their block with

luck in Moosomin, arriving here in June, '83 . . . Mr. Smithers has succeeded in working up a thriving business, is a good citizen, honest dealer, and with commendable foresight has established a business which emphatically says, 'We are here to stay.'"

Whether he stayed or not is unknown: few facts about and no memory of John Smithers remain in Moo-

somin today. One of the rare documents attesting to his presence is an 1897 certificate of title showing that Mary Hannah Smithers, wife of John Smithers, bought an entire block of land in Moosomin from William Bain Scarth of Winnipeg, a trustee of the Canada North-West Land Company, Limited. This was the company that sold Canadian Pacific Railway

maple trees, the Prices named their new home The Maples.

Kenneth Price, an English immigrant who had been joined in the North-West Territories by his parents, had farmed at Cannington until his house burned down. He then drove stage, raced horses, and played tennis and cricket at Moosomin before settling down to become postmaster after he married and had seven children.

The property he bought from the Smitherses was impressive, and the house charming. It was also deceptively spacious. Supplementing its cottage style and proportions are two broad bays, as well as wide gables rising on three sides of its truncated hip roof, all of which contributed space and light to the expansive rooms inside. The home was also well appointed, with stained glass in three windows, and a fireplace faced with squares of white marble and three classic figures in sculpted relief.

Phyllis, who eventually taught kindergarten classes and cared for her widowed father in the house, paints a quaint picture of her

childhood there. The grand piano, for example, came with the parlour, and it was here that her mother, an admired vocalist in local operas, practised for roles and Phyllis prepared for music lessons. She also tells of walking home from skating at dusk, following the town's lamplighter as he ignited the tops of the light standards with his long-handled torch.

Phyllis's father had her promise never to sell The Maples, but she was unable to keep that promise. So the piano and the spindled staircase she dusted every Saturday – and certainly the lamplighter – are long gone, and the maple-lined estate is now filled with other houses.

The detailed brickwork surrounding the main windows and doors is carried on for the smaller dormer windows, including the segmented arch.

But mica still glitters from millions of points in the squared granite, and the well-maintained house and its landscaped surroundings have recently been framed by a Victorian-style wrought-iron fence. The Maples remains well-loved. ❧

No two sides of this house have the same design. The south wall includes a small bay and the largest massing of stonework, which clearly shows the coursing employed in building the Smithers house.

The Bruce Residence

SASKATOON

Although it's one of Saskatoon's most attractive homes on one of Saskatoon's most attractive streets, the house built by Henry A. Bruce in 1912 is more than just a pretty face. Like beautiful women of a certain age, it has its secrets. ❧ And its linage is impeccable: the land on which it was built was first owned by the founders of Saskatoon, the Temperance Colonization Society. Subsequent owners included Archibald and Russell Wilson, the latter a school trustee in the final years of the original Victoria School, and eventually the mayor of Saskatoon. It was the Wilsons who subdivided the quarter-section they'd bought from the Society, allowing broker Henry Bruce to buy the 100-foot (30 m) frontage in 1912. ❧ Unfortunately, no further details are available: neither the source of the

A flared roof over the gable window is an attractive topping over the front entrance to the house.

home's design nor the builder is known. The design source is particularly intriguing, as the house is unique in Saskatoon. Architectural historian Leslie Maitland describes it as "an Arts and Crafts inspired house with a Rustic interpretation . . . a very Canadian marriage of the two styles," and the book she co-authored, *A Guide to Architectural Styles,* supports that suggestion with its description of buildings influenced by the Arts and Crafts movement.

"Like the English rural cottages that they imitated, their appeal lay in the bold composition of projecting volumes, steeply pitched roofs and massive and irregularly placed chimneys; and their low, ground-hugging contours, suggesting that they had been rooted in place for centuries . . . The movement sought to create buildings that had the rightness to place and the sense of belonging characteristic of vernacular architecture."

The Rustic influence is identified by the uncut fieldstone on the chimney and veranda, a common feature of early wilderness-park buildings such as those at Banff,

Jasper, and, closer to home, Manitou Lake. Designed to blend with the environment, the Rustic style was an ideal amalgam for the Bruce home, located on the banks of the South Saskatchewan River. The veranda, which is also lined with uncut fieldstone, was originally open, encouraging an intimacy with the environment that was real as well as stylistic.

Although the rusticity was carried inside as well – the massive fireplace in the living room is of fieldstone – the Arts and Crafts influence predominates: oak dados, ceiling beams, and generous woodwork, as well as small, leaded-glass window panes. Adding to the cozy ambience are built-in benches and three more fireplaces.

Such attention to detail suggests the house was the builder's dream home, but it was nevertheless sold in 1916 to New Brunswick-born Dr. Harold Alexander. He had arrived in Saskatoon from post-graduate work in New York the same year the house was built, and married an Ontario woman in 1913. It was during the Alexander years, which extended until shortly after Dr. Alexander died in 1942, that the house blossomed.

In 1926, an attached garage with a style-sensitive, second-storey addition above was constructed, and around it the Alexanders created an English-style garden, complete with a pond, terracing, stone paths, and a high-backed garden seat within an arbour. They also raised four children, one of whom became the first female doctor in the Canadian Navy and then married a man who became the chief executive officer of Alcan. Another daughter, a dietitian, married Russell (Rusty) Macdonald, editor of *The Western Producer*.

It has been said that behind every exceptional daughter is an exceptional father, and Dr. Alexander qualified. In addition to his work as surgical chief of staff at St. Paul's Hospital, he bred award-winning Belgian horses and raised shorthorn cattle and Yorkshire pigs at his farm twenty-three kilometres north of Saskatoon. The bones of two left legs uncovered in the garden during recent excavations, however, were human: after a forensic examination, the police concluded, "The doctor brought his homework home."

And when the doctor himself died, the home began a gradual decline. The property was divided, the garden was lost, doors and woodwork on the second floor were removed, and walls and floors were covered.

Then, in November 2000, Ward and Annette Stebner arrived. Researching both history and period building and decorating techniques, they have been working towards a restoration of the home to the Alexander era ever since. Ward, for example, has learned how to replicate the sand-finish of the walls lining the stairs and upper hall, and he fumes all the oak needed to replace the original woodwork on the second floor. To ensure that the new cedar shingles were installed in the original style, he instructed the roofing contractors on how to carry out a Boston weave. He doesn't plan to reconnect the maid's call system, but every other original detail receives his enthusiastic and educated attention.

Still, he cautions, "We're passionate about the house, but we're only custodians."

"We're all temporary. The house will still be here long after we're gone," Annette explains. "We're looking after it so that others can enjoy it as much as we do." ❧

Initially, the veranda was an open-air feature of the house. (Saskatchewan Archives Board, Regina Album, c. 1914 – photo 15)

The Kinsey House

MOOSOMIN

Amos Kinsey was a character, no doubt about it. But was he the first owner of the restored and renovated fieldstone house on Moosomin's main street? Irrefutable proof is yet to be found. ❧ Proof of Amos is everywhere, however. When the Canadian Pacific Railway reached what became Moosomin in 1882, for example, an early traveller wrote about spending the night in one of the hastily erected hotels. Of his thirty roommates – everyone slept in one big room, where "The beds were represented by a pile of blankets in one corner and everyone was his own chamber maid" – nine were remembered by name. One was Amos. ❧ Amos's daughter, writing in *Moosomin Century One*, states that he was born of a Quaker family who had moved from the United States to Ontario. He came west

The front of the house reveals the large and colourful stones used in the building's primary façade, as well as the extensive pale yellow brick quoins.

against his parents' wishes — they feared they'd never see him again, and there is no evidence their fears were unfounded – and established a homestead at Cannington, where he remained for three years. Here, according to local history, he trained two elk to pull a cart.

No grass grew under his feet in Moosomin either. By the summer of 1888 he had become a *Moosomin Courier* staple, noted for grading Main Street, losing a horse due to "inflammation of the intestine," and advertising "a great bargain," a Gordon Street house and lot for sale at $300 each. He also operated a freight delivery business, and according to his daughter, bought lots on Main Street, and "took over the rooming and boarding part of the first Queen's Hotel."

And then, in the 1892 *Moosomin Courier,* are two items that likely established the

accepted date for the house on Main Street: in June it was reported that "Mr. Amos Kinsey has had plans drawn by Mr. T. Grayson for a neat little stone cottage on Main Street"; and in September that year "Mr. Amos Kinsey is building a very neat stone residence on Main Street."

Although described with wide-ranging epithets today, Amos was well liked in his day. A February 1896 *Moosomin Spectator* reported that "Mr. A. Kinsey and Miss Nellie Allan, two of Moosomin's most popular young people, were married on Wednesday evening the 5th inst., at 8:30 with the Rev. J. A. Reddon at the residence of the groom." Amos was thirty-eight.

Good news and bad then followed in quick succession: his first daughter was born in 1897, his second in 1898, and his wife died in 1899. The youngest daughter was taken to Wapella to live with her aunt, but died of scarlet fever in 1904.

According to the surviving daughter, she and her father eventually moved to a "little house on the farm Father had on the west edge of town."

Meanwhile, the Lough family arrived in Moosomin in 1905, bought the house credited to Amos, and sold it in 1913.

The uncertainty about this home's original owner and construction date is due to a legal paper trail that doesn't show Amos Kinsey's name until 1917. The house and its corner lot were subsequently sold and resold and finally taken over by the Town of Moosomin for unpaid taxes. Its ownership by a well-known Moosomin family, the Tanners, began in 1944 and lasted until 1998, during which time it gained a rear addition and renewed respect.

It is a worthy recipient of that respect. The large squared stones, especially those on the sides presented to the intersecting streets, have been carefully cut, positioned, and mortared in regular, neat courses of unvaried width. The brickwork is of similar high quality, with wide quoins, shallow arches made of three rows of bricks over the first-floor windows, and a precise round arch over the front door. The composition of stone and brick at the front entrance is clearly the work of an artist.

The Kinsey house was surrounded with a page-wire fence and trees shortly after it was completed. By the time of this photo, which includes the Lough children, those trees had matured sufficiently to virtually obscure the fine masonry details. (Marie and Dennis Everett)

The stonemason credited with this work is the elusive George Dalgleish, the same man who allegedly built the Smithers house in Moosomin. Confirmation cannot be found, but both houses were unquestionably built by the same person. The glistening stones were likely found in the same area as well, although some are jet black in this two-storey home and the reds are even richer and more abundant than in the Smithers house.

Little wonder travellers stop to take pictures. With or without the colourful Amos Kinsey, it is a showpiece. 🌾

A close examination of the windows and doors reveals the brick quoins and triple row of bricks used to construct the segmented arches.

Town & Country Schools

Adults petitioned for the early schools of Saskatchewan, served as their trustees, and taught, met, and danced in them, but it is the voices of children that lingers in their stone walls. That's why these empty buildings, mostly found in rural Saskatchewan, look so sad, so lonely, so abandoned. Even Victoria School, now at the heart of the University of Saskatchewan, stands alone and cold, but still echoing with youthful laughter.

Saskatchewan's homesteaders and urban pioneers clearly placed a high priority on education in their society. From the small one-room schools to the larger two-storey multiple-class complexes, schools have featured prominently in the development of the province. Local history books feature major chapters devoted to education, often including details for every small school ever erected in the district. ❧ In towns and villages, these small schools were quickly replaced with larger structures as the population increased. In some instances, new schools replaced earlier structures less than a decade after the initial construction. Sometimes the earlier schools were reused elsewhere in the community; in other cases they were simply demolished to make way for the newer and larger edifices. ❧ As with other

Constructed about 1903, the Weyburn Public School also served as a church and as a meeting hall for the community. Such multiple uses were quite common at a time when it was too costly to erect separate facilities. (Soo Line Historical Museum, Weyburn)

pioneer constructions, many initial school buildings were of frame construction, to be replaced later with more elaborate masonry structures, either of brick or stone. In both instances, the larger buildings not only provided greater space for students and school activities, they also often reflected the community interest in building safer structures, including improved fire escapes and more extensive use of fire retardant products.

Schools, like churches, were also local landmarks, and evoked a sense of pride throughout the entire community. Official openings could become major social events, and the school itself often fulfilled non-educational community needs, such as temporary quarters for religious services, seasonal community gatherings, dances, and election polling stations. In times of extreme need, they also served as places of refuge or, as was the case during the Spanish flu epidemic of 1918, as makeshift hospitals.

Schools were also a place to instruct students on some of the finer classical details of architecture. Hence, for larger urban schools, one would find columns with all of the basic features, such as bases and capitals, lintels and sills, keystones and quoins, as well as pediments and different types of arches over doors and windows. Such refinement was more common in eastern than western Canada, but in many prairie schools teachers could discuss the history of classical construction, and then point out some of those features in the very building where the students were taught.

Although a substantial number of Saskatchewan schools were made of stone, many have been destroyed or, like homes and commercial buildings, have been significantly renovated. Many more, particularly the one-room structures, now stand abandoned, as school consolidation over the past half century has made these structures obsolete. In fact, the ongoing centralization of both urban and rural schools has resulted even in the closure of some major urban facilities. More often than not, these older masonry schools are demolished rather than reintegrated into the community for some alternate viable function. Some exceptions exist, but a review of community histories show how many fine school build-

Collegiate Institute (later renamed Central Collegiate), Regina was a classical history teacher's delight, displaying various architectural features and stone elements (c. 1927). (Saskatchewan Archives Board R-A 33,580)

ings have been demolished in the past quarter century. Those that have been preserved are generally removed from the educational system and are now used as community museums or as some other cultural or recreational facility.

Three of the four schools featured in this section lack the elements of formal architectural design and are therefore said to portray a vernacular design. Indeed, some, like the Orkney and Victoria schools, were designed by local stonemasons. However, the larger Summerberry School shows the kinds of detail often incorporated by professional architects. ❧

Yorkton's first school, a small one-room stone structure constructed in 1890, was certainly no larger than many of its rural counterparts. (City of Yorkton Archives-Jackson Collection – *YJ-03781*)

OPPOSITE: The truncated hip roof on
Summerberry School is a prominent feature,
while the yellow brick quoins at the corners
and surrounding the doors and windows
highlight those essential building features.

Public School

SUMMERBERRY

Surely no other school in Saskatchewan was as reviled by Department of Education inspectors as the 1886 one-room frame structure in Summerberry. ❧ In September 1907, for example, the department's deputy commissioner wrote to the secretary of School District 33, "I regret to inform you that an Inspector's report shows that your school building and school accommodation generally are inadequate to the needs of your district. Thus it would appear that the school building is altogether too small and a second teacher is needed. Further, it is said that the closets are in disgraceful condition." ❧ He concluded with the warning that failure to respond to the needs of the students would leave the district open to forfeiture of government grants. ❧ In August the following year, another school

The south side of Summerberry School has no windows, indicating where the blackboards were located.

inspector's report stated, "It is well-nigh criminal to allow children to be educated under such circumstances in an old, well-established English-speaking community."

Contrary to the inspectors' impressions, however, the trustees of Summerberry Protestant School District (its name until 1931) were neither negligent nor uncaring. In February 1908, the school board's secretary/treasurer wrote of the intention "to build a school far in excess of our present needs as it is to be in the village and we are afraid

if we do not do this, in the course of ten or fifteen years the school would be too small. Consequently we are building a good village school of solid stone, similar to the Sintaluta School at an estimated Ten Thousand Dollars . . ."

The very next month, the trade magazine *Construction* announced: "Architect Victor M. [sic] Horwood, Winnipeg, Man., has prepared plans and will shortly receive tenders for the construction of a two-storey four-roomed solid stone schoolhouse to be erected in Summerberry, Sask." Victor W.

Horwood, who had designed the 1906/07 school at Sintaluta, later became Manitoba's provincial architect.

The school's completion was noted in a short "Summerberry" item in the June 3, 1909 Grenfell *Sun:* "Mr. Talmay of Wapella is finishing the painting and masonry on the new school and is going to build the stable. The latter is of stone and was partly built this fall."

Richard Talmay farmed near Rocanville northeast of Wapella, and is credited with building many fieldstone buildings in Grenfell, all of which are distinguished by their brick quoining of the corners, doors, and windows. The bricks of the quoins at Summerberry School, as revealed by an October 1908 lien on the property, originated at Manitoba's Stephens Brick Company Ltd.

The interior was divided into two classrooms on the first floor, where grades one to ten were taught by two teachers, and an auditorium on the second, where dances, concerts, social gatherings, and Sunday school were held. In 1922, when grades eleven and twelve were added, the auditorium became a classroom where grades nine to twelve were taught by the principal. The basement had a toilet for girls and, eventually, for boys, and a large room for games such as pump-pump-pull-away during inclement weather.

Eventually, however, dwindling enrollments forced closure of the high school classes, with these students being bused to Wolseley. On August 1, 1963, Summerberry S.D. 33 was officially "disorga-nized," and all students were bused to Wolseley.

But statistics do not tell the whole story of any school building, the one suggested by the ringing laughter and shouts of schoolyards every-where. And, paradoxically, it is the joyless school inspec-tors' reports that reveal this aspect of Summerberry School. In 1930, for example, one scolded, "The order in the halls should be improved. What I heard may not be a daily occurrence but it was boisterous." Two years later, another wrote, "I suggest that more attention be paid to the discipline in the halls. I am inclined to think there is some vaulting over the stair railing."

Former student June Wagman just laughs when she hears of these reports. They could have been written in the 1940s and 1950s, when her own memories were being formed. And these memories are why, after the school had been empty for nineteen years, she bought it in 1985. "I just loved the school. The town itself meant so much to me and the school was part of that."

June and her husband, Neil, have re-created black-boards with paint and found old wooden and cast-iron desks to replace the originals. A former teacher, she has dec-orated with her own teaching aids, and piled outdated school texts on the desks. In preparation for two reunions at the school, she hung lists of all the students from 1914 to

1963 and prepared posters with their photographs. She and Neil even moved a small trailer onto the schoolyard for their "summer retreat."

But they don't use the trailer anymore: "The elevators are all gone," she explains, retelling the tale of rural Saskatchewan and also of the schools that were the other centre of the community. "It's too lonely now." ❧

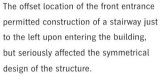

The offset location of the front entrance permitted construction of a stairway just to the left upon entering the building, but seriously affected the symmetrical design of the structure.

The interior of the school still displays classrooms much as they were when the school was in full operation.

Hearts of Oak School

NEAR REDVERS

One-room schoolhouses are the last living link with Saskatchewan's pioneer days. Some were built shortly after the first homesteaders arrived in the 1880s, some remained open until the late 1960s, and during that span, little changed. Most were inadequately heated by a wood-burning stove and dimly lit by lanterns. ❧ Memories of these schools are still vivid and stories still told: "I remember riding to school when it was so cold. Too cold," recalls Albert Laval, who entered grade one at Hearts of Oak School sixteen kilometres northwest of Redvers in 1952. "I cried, and the tears froze on my cheeks. Then I told myself to smarten up. It was almost as cold when I got inside the school anyway." ❧ The main difference between Albert's memories and those of hundreds of others is the composition of his

The careful selection and placement of the stones by the stonemason is evident in the construction of the front of the Hearts of Oak School.

school's walls: most were frame and some were brick, but few besides Hearts of Oak were stone.

The reason for the stones of Hearts of Oak was twofold: Billy Good, a stonemason, lived on the same quarter as the school in the early years; and, as reported by another Hearts of Oak alumnus, John Madsen, "Rocks were the most plentiful building material in the area. We spent two weeks every year picking them."

Hearts of Oak School District #1831 also stirs up other differences, these concerning the year it originated. Some say they have books stamped with "Hearts of Oak, District of Assiniboia," which date it to before Saskatchewan became a province in 1905, while Department of Education documents indicate the school district was organized July 23, 1907, and the site for the building of Hearts of Oak was approved in October 1907.

Difference of opinion is nothing new to Hearts of Oak. Included in the Department of Education's file, for example, is a handwritten, unsigned "Notice" from a seemingly disgruntled ratepayer who couldn't spell: "Another unlawful anuel school meeting at no. 1831 S.D. in 1912. A paper catcher." This had been attached to the official Jan. 2, 1912 report on a poorly attended and thus "unsatisfactory" annual meeting.

Still, the school was welcomed by the men and women who homesteaded the area after the Canadian Pacific Railway laid tracks about fifteen kilometres south in 1901. Stonemason Billy Good and his father, in fact, were two of the first to arrive. So, when the school was being considered, Billy's father submitted a hand-drawn map to the Department of Education, pointing out the sloughs, low land, high land, and "low land but not wet" areas in the sections around the potential sites. He was describing what geologists now call a postglacial "knob and kettle" landscape.

The school John's son built on the highest "knob" is still

beautiful in its simplicity, including the no-nonsense craftsmanship of its masonry. All the grey, rust and yellow stones are squared and laid in courses of about the same width from top to bottom. Because mortar was used sparingly, the careful cutting and fitting is evident: Billy Good obviously believed, as did other master stonemasons of that era, that a wall should not rely solely on mortar to keep it straight, upright, and maybe even eternal.

The sills and straight lintels of the eight windows and one door are of concrete, as is the broad, half-metre-high deck across the full front of the school. Alumni remember the deck as home base for tag, and the perfect place to mount their horse for the ride home.

Horses spent the day in the school barn, where each family stored feed in their assigned manger. The barn is gone now, as are the outhouses, separate ones for boys and girls. Inside, the metal ceiling is intact, but the blackboards and Station Agent wood-burning stove are gone. And only pieces and pedals of the Kentsman organ remain on

the scratched and dirty fir floor, once varnished every year before school started.

But just ask and it's all back: the desks with folding seats that pinched; the Christmas concerts when fathers would pump the dimming lanterns; frozen lunches or milk jostled into butter by the end of the horseback trip to school; the welcome sight of the school on a frosty morning and the even more welcome sight of smoke rising from the chimney.

Because of the influx of Danes into the area in the 1920s, some memories have a Scandinavian hue: adults who took English lessons at the school, Lutheran church services at the school in the sum-

mer, and evergreen branches hung over the entrance for special events.

One of John Madsen's stories strikes a universal chord, however: "I loved the warm spring days when the windows were open and I could hear the wrens. I wished I was anywhere but there." 🦅

When newly completed, Hearts of Oak School boldly displayed its stone construction and crisp mortar lines, projecting a strong horizontal line. (Saskatchewan Archives Board R-A 20,594)

A potbelly stove provided the only heat for the students and teacher – too hot if you were close by, too cold if you were further away.

Mount Joy School

NEAR GLASNEVIN

Perhaps it's the commanding position on an empty slope above the road. Perhaps it's the aristocratically steep roof, tall windows touching the eaves as if raised in unquestioned superiority. The glass in those windows may be broken and a north wall may be a heap of stones, but Mount Joy School retains the aura of a building once considered too fine to serve as a lowly country school. ❧ The first homesteaders in this area northwest of Ogema began arriving about 1908 and, by 1911, there were enough of them to call a meeting to organize a school district. By March the following year, the Department of Education had agreed, but it balked at approving the design for the school itself: a fieldstone building with a full basement and furnace, and a fieldstone "entrance hall or lobby" with broad stairs up to the

The quality of construction for the less-visible back wall is noticeably inferior, as evidenced by the use of a variety of sizes and shapes of stone.

single classroom, and two sets of narrow stairs to the basement.

"In this connection I may say that it is questionable if a rural district would be justified in erecting such an elaborate building. I may say that it is not usual for a rural district to put in a full basement and furnace . . ." wrote the deputy minister. His letter also objected to the stairs because of the danger to smaller children and the propensity for dust collection. The entrance hall would be cold and draughty, further-

more, and where were the cloakrooms?

When the Mount Joy School District # 341 trustees did not respond, the Education Department raised another objection: because the proposed stone building was not located in the exact centre of the district, the boundaries would likely change, so a school of such "a permanent nature" would be unwise.

That did it. The trustees' immediate reply stated that the proposed location was as close to the exact centre as

possible, and that the building material was chosen because of "the quantity of stone handy," a saving for taxpayers. Six days later, the Education Department granted permission to erect the proposed school.

The "quantity of stone handy" is still illustrated by boulders in stone piles on adjacent fields. Darryl Wiles, who farms his grandfather's homestead two kilometres down the road, ruefully explains that the school is within a three-kilometre-wide ridge of extremely stony land, a "stagnant ice moraine" in geological terms.

Darryl's grandfather was among those who gathered and hauled the granite and sandstone from this moraine, and three local farmers helped the stonemason, G. Stothers, cut and lay them in a coursed style. Mr. Stothers, of whom nothing is known, exhibited little imagination – only the stones of the slightly arched lintels above the basement windows indicate an eye for colour and symmetry – but three walls indicate he knew his craft. His helpers likely laid the uneven and ill-sorted back wall.

Mount Joy School first opened its door to students in grades one to eight in October 1912, and soon became the social hub of the community as well. First was the Christmas concert and, a few days later, an oyster supper, both intended to raise money for a school organ. But the oyster supper lost money and the trustees used the proceeds from the Christmas concert to pay the debt. The teacher was furious; spittin' mad, it might have been said, if she hadn't been such a lady.

Helen Clark, born in 1917, was not around for that first oyster supper, but she does remember those that followed: "I couldn't stomach them," she says of the delicacies relished raw or in soup by her family and neighbours. She recalls other occasions with greater fondness: the picnics, dances, pie socials and winter evenings when families would arrive by horse and sleigh to play whist, dance, break for midnight lunch, and dance some more. "The Wiles were musical," she explains, referring to the violins and banjos of Darryl's grandfather, uncles and cousins, " . . . and when the

little ones fell asleep they were laid in those broad windowsills."

Helen makes no mention of the homebrew that enlivened some evenings. "It was kept outside. Lots of it," says another former student of almost equal age. "The guys would have a drink and come in feeling frisky."

Darryl, although too young to know about the homebrew, remembers the babies in windowsills, chasing girls with mice he caught in the horse barn, and the furnace. Always the furnace. It's a vivid memory for generations of male students enlisted as caretakers: the way it smoked; the opportunities it provided to escape class; the frozen horseback ride to school on dark winter mornings to get it started.

That furnace remains, its stern visage intact, in the basement. It just needs a little kindling, some coal. "Once you got the old girl heated up, it was good for the day," says Darryl, who was tending it when the school closed in 1959. He'd still do it too. And have the wall repaired, replace the windows, and evict the swallows and raccoons. "If I had a million dollars . . ." ❧

The triple roof and set-back as the extensions reduce in size add extra character to this fine stone structure.

A close-up examination of the school reveals the regular courses of fieldstone and the careful selection of stone colours for the segmented arches over the basement windows

Places of Worship

Histories of fieldstone churches may seem a dry topic to everyone but members of their congregations, many of which no longer exist. But they document life: the bride climbing through the window of a locked church during a sudden rain; the church organist playing for his own wedding; the fly that buzzes at church windows during every summer service since glass was invented; and the horses of a priest that "will be remembered much longer" than their owner's sermons. Still, it's not all fun: there is also the sorrow of mental illness and deaths before their time.

OPPOSITE: St. Raphael's Roman Catholic Church, erected in 1914 at Cantal, displays prominent stone buttresses at the corners and along the side walls. Its bell tower is small in comparison, and of a design that may be unique in the province.

T he two most common stone structures to survive in Saskatchewan are farmhouses and churches. Of these, the latter tend to be the best preserved, as congregations were not as prone to making alterations and renovations as private property owners. Nevertheless, some religious structures have been modified over the years to better address the climatic and lighting needs of the congregation, or to accommodate those who had difficulty with the innumerable steps often featured at the front entrance. ❧ Stone churches also spoke to the sense of permanence in a community, and the need to build for the future as well as the present. Unlike today, pioneers built for a hundred or two hundred years. These religious monuments were built, as various datestones and brass plaques attest, "To the Glory of God." Churches also

Rev. T. A. Teitlebaum assisting Bishop Anson *(centre)* in laying the cornerstone at St. Augustine's Anglican Church, Saltcoats, 1892. (Saskatchewan Archives Board R-A 20,727)

FAR RIGHT: The final design of St. Thomas shows some of the changes made to the original plans, shown on the following page. (Saskatchewan Archives Board R-A 21,376)

serve as community landmarks, whether in an urban or rural setting, and are often used by local residents to provide directions to people visiting the area. They are also points of interest that, in many instances, reflect the community's initial establishment. Often they are the oldest surviving buildings in the region.

While virtually all denominations erected stone places of worship, the inventory of such structures indicates that the largest number were built by Anglicans, particularly at the turn of the twentieth cen-

tury, sometimes, but not always, replacing earlier frame or log buildings.

Today, at the start of the twenty-first century, a disturbing number of these long-surviving landmarks of our pioneer era are being abandoned due to the decrease in the number of parishioners, amalgamation with other congregations, the real or perceived high cost of operation and maintenance, or simply a desire by the present generation to worship in a "modern" church.

Many country churches were designed with limited formal planning, and often consisted of rough sketches and minimal written instruction. At times it involved the work of a trained architect,

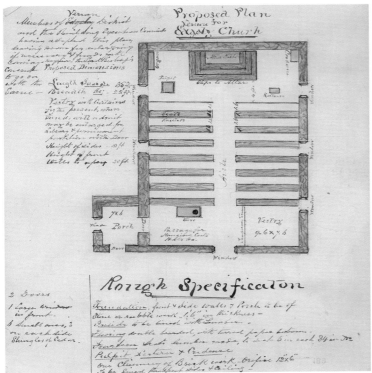

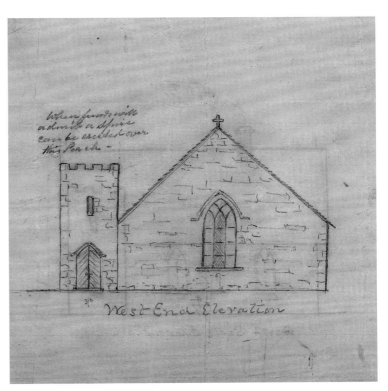

but more often than not, these buildings were designed and erected by a local carpenter, stonemason, or bricklayer. Few such plans have survived, but those that have provide an interesting insight into the sparse directions that were provided to the builders. Final details were regularly left up to their own craftsmanship and talents. In addition to the fine exterior architectural designs found in stone churches, these historic structures often also include delicate interior details, well-crafted furnishings, and superb stained glass windows. ❧

LEFT: A drawing showing the proposed layout for St. Thomas Anglican Church, Vernon, near McLean. (Saskatchewan Archives Board R-705, file VII.204b)

RIGHT: A drawing showing the proposed tower and west window detail. (Saskatchewan Archives Board R-705, file VII.204a)

OPPOSITE: St. Thomas Anglican Church incorporates some traditional ecclesiastical design elements, such as the crenellated corner tower, the pointed arch windows, and the placement of crosses at both ends of the gable roof.

St. Thomas (Vernon) Anglican Church

NEAR MCLEAN

The history of St. Thomas Anglican Church, Vernon, begins with one of Saskatchewan's bonanza farms, Edgeley Farm, located on 11,520 acres of land northwest of Qu'Appelle. Established by the Sykes Brothers of Manchester the same year as the better-known Bell Farm at Indian Head, 1882, Edgeley Farm was named after a hamlet next to the Scottish home of one of the brothers. ❧ The Sykes brothers sent out William Cameron to manage their farm, and in 1888, William married Emily Winter of England. A month later, Anglican services began in the Edgeley Farm dining hall, often officiated by theological students from St. John's College near Qu'Appelle. ❧ Meanwhile, back in England, gentleman farmer William Cooper had lost everything due to hoof and mouth disease of his cattle. With eleven

The cemetery at St. Thomas Church, situated directly east of the building, helps provide a peaceful ambiance for this picturesque stone structure. The cross on William Cooper's grave is visible in the centre background, metres away from the church he helped to build.

children to feed, he and his wife decided to emigrate, and joined Lord Brassey's Church Colonization Society just east of Qu'Appelle in 1889.

Because he found forty acres too little to support his large family, and because he was ill-prepared for any real farm work, Cooper soon left the settlement to open a restaurant in Indian Head. But then his wife died, and a few months later, two of his daughters married local men while he was away. Upset at their deception and again destitute, he was saved by his Liverpool cousin, Sir William Vernon, nephew of Bishop Anson, first bishop of the Diocese of Qu'Appelle. Sir William bought a quarter-section of land with a home-steader's house for William.

By this time, the district was becoming increasingly settled and it became more convenient to hold the Anglican services southwest of

Edgeley Farm at William's farm, now called Vernon Bluff.

"It was William Cooper and Mrs. Cameron who were instrumental in establishing a permanent church," continues Bruce Farrer, William Cooper's great-grandson. "About half of its projected cost was donated through the efforts of Mrs. Cameron's mother in England, and Sir William donated a few acres of his quarter section for its location."

According to the diocesan publication *Qu'Appelle Occasional Papers,* the cornerstone, "a handsome piece of granite found on the Edgeley Farm," was laid on July 28, 1898 by Bishop Grisdale, third bishop of the Qu'Appelle Diocese.

Stonemason Ludvig Monson of Fort Qu'Appelle and carpenter J. B. Robinson and painter A. H. Hollingshead of Qu'Appelle Station were hired to build the church. To do so, they followed three pages of anonymously hand-drawn and coloured sketches. The proposed plan shows a rectangle with an inside length of 35 feet and breadth of 25 feet (10.5 m × 7.5 m), and includes information such as, "front and side walls & Porch to be of stone or rubble work 1'6" [half metre] in thickness," and "Inside to be lined with Lumber." The flooring was to be "double boarded, with tarred paper between." The exterior drawings offered two choices for the west elevation: three peaked windows; and one large pointed-arch window and, at the base of a crenellated Norman-style tower, the main entrance. Above the tower was written, "When funds will admit a Spire can be erected over this Porch."

The present church indicates that funds were never found for a spire, and also that the proposed plan was not followed exactly: the entrance in the tower faces north, and the west window is small and round-arched. The interior of the present church is partly explained by the building committee's undated report: a chancel and permanent vestry were to be added when funds were made available but, in the meantime, "provision has been made for building a chancel by having an archway built in the east wall of the church."

Consecration of the church by Bishop Grisdale took place September 29, 1899.

In 1903, the stone vestry and chancel were added, at which time a round stained-glass window featuring a bleeding pelican was installed behind the oak altar. This altar had been shipped from a studio in Stratford on Avon, England, where it had been designed and carved by the mother of the first organist. The reredos – an ornamental screen covering the wall at the back of the altar – was designed and painted especially for Vernon Church by the organist's English cousin. The pulpit and the ornate gilded-iron chandelier, which supported kerosene lamps, were donated by the Anglican Pro-Cathedral at Qu'Appelle.

The kerosene lamps were stolen in the 1960s, so candles are now lit for the annual Christmas Eve service. Regular services are also held every second Sunday from Easter until Thanksgiving. Bruce Farrer plays the organ for these services, as he has done since 1961. He also played for his own wedding, the bap-

LEFT: Deep window wells help frame the stained glass windows.

BELOW: The ornate brass chandelier suspended from the wooden ceiling was a gift from St. Peter's Anglican Church, Qu'Appelle, then serving as the Pro-Cathedral of the Diocese of Qu'Appelle.

tisms of all of his children and grandchildren, and the funerals of his parents.

"Now," says Bruce, "For my own funeral . . ." 🌿

OPPOSITE: Orkney Presbyterian Church became part of the United Church of Canada in 1925. The irregular stone coursing provides a pleasing contrast with the wooden components of the building.

Orkney Presbyterian Church & School

NEAR YORKTON

As with most pioneer places of worship, the Orkney Presbyterian Church was a community effort. According to the 1924 book *Ox Trails to Highways*, however, one of the volunteers digging the foundation trenches was a Roman Catholic who predicted that the church wouldn't last long because it was built on a "Catholic foundation." ❧ That was in the spring of 1893, and the Orkney church has not only stood for more than a hundred years, it will likely stand another hundred. The same can be said for the 1897 Orkney School across the road. ❧ The unlikely genesis of these sturdy structures was the Toronto-based York Farmers' Colonization Company, the formation of which had been encouraged by the Dominion government. Offering 160 acres free to homesteaders, and selling

The restored Orkney Church *(left)* and School.

established by the company but renamed Yorkton in 1884. (Six years later, the townsite was relocated about four kilometres south.) He wintered in Manitoba, wrote his mother and brothers advising them to emigrate, and returned to his land to build a log cabin the following spring. And on the day his extended family and four other Scotsmen arrived, a new sound was heard in that land: the skirl of bagpipes.

Although their lives were full with breaking the land, building homes, and even defending their families during the North-West Rebellion, the Orkney settlers never neglected their religious life. Church was held in their homes, their log school and a boarding house in York City. By 1891, however, they elected the first official church board of the Orkney Presbyterian congregation. John Reid was one of the members and remained so for forty years.

Although the congregation could not even raise the $100 for an ordained minister in the summer months, and was told a stone church would be $150 more than a wooden church of the same size, stone

odd-numbered sections of land to companies for resale, the government hoped to promote settlement in the North-West Territories, while the company hoped to do this and turn a profit too.

Within two months of the company's May 1882 incorporation, four York officials visited an area around what is now the city of Yorkton and bought the odd-numbered sections in six townships. More land was bought the following year. Advertising the land at $2 per acre, the company promised to build roads, set up businesses, operate

stagecoaches and a ferry across the Qu'Appelle River, and offer credit for three years without interest.

The response was immediate, and among the settlers who arrived that summer was John Reid of Eday, one of the Orkney Islands north of Scotland. His father had been killed in a farm accident, his mother and three siblings had been deposed by their laird, and John eventually moved to Edinburgh to apprentice to a cabinetmaker. Here he read of the free land in the Canadian North-West.

The land John chose was west of York City, a hamlet

was chosen. In 1893, the cornerstone of Orkney Presbyterian church was laid on land donated by the York Farmers' Colonization Company.

According to the book *Orkney Stones 1882–1989* by the Orkney Historical Society,

The stones were gathered and hauled from nearby areas (which to this day are still very stoney) and hauled to the building site with ox-drawn stoneboats and wagons.

The limestone was quarried from the Smith Brothers farm. The lime making operation involved considerable night work to keep the fires burning in the kiln. Firewood was also hauled in to make certain that fires wouldn't die.

Stones and mortar were wheeled in wooden wheelbarrows and when the walls became higher, up ramps, to the stonemason, N. H. Neilson. He cut and shaped all the stones. Men also carried mortar and some stones in hods slung over their shoulders.

Volunteers built a frame porch and, inside, a half-metre-high, two-metre-deep platform at the north end. The paneled pulpit, as well as "all the fine woodwork," was built by William Rendall, John Reid's father-in-law, a cabinetmaker from Orkney. Incised on William's 1896 gravestone, the second to be erected in the adjacent Orkney Church cemetery, is the epitaph "The Pulpit Builder."

With church union in 1925, Orkney Presbyterian Church became the Orkney United Church.

When the church was officially declared a municipal heritage property in 1982, its architectural style was described as "strongly reminiscent of churches and schools in western and northern Scotland with finely cut stone walls and little ornamentation." The same words can be applied to Orkney School, also a municipal heritage property.

The present Orkney School was built in 1897 to replace the original log school that formed the core of Orkney Protestant Public School District #97. It was almost identical in size and shape to the church, but the

Students in front of Orkney School, 1897. (*Orkney Stones 1882–1989*, The Orkney Historical Society)

porch was built of stone and the lintels are stone slabs instead of wooden beams. The stonemason was again the Norwegian Nels Holor Neilson.

The Orkney School Board, on which John Reid served for thirty years, acquired the Orkney church as a second classroom in 1939. By the mid-1940s, the stone school was empty and, in 1958, classes in the church ended as well. Both buildings remained unused, but were restored in 1984 and, as testimony to their status in the community, have been immaculately maintained ever since. Today, in fact, they look as if they were built yesterday. ❧

Christ Anglican Church

WAPELLA

Sounds and smells, not documents and date stones, often tell the real story of any building. ❧ "The buzz of the fly that seemed to attend every summer service and beat against the window," for example, is one nugget in the "Memories" page of Wapella's Christ Anglican Church history. "The smell of the sip of communion wine on my parents' breath," wrote another parishioner, while yet another remembered "the clatter of dropped hymn books, the dull clonk of an overturned kneeler." ❧ Then there's the equally evocative "smell of the hot rubber as we warmed ourselves on the furnace register on cold winter days and burned our overshoes." This memory can be dated, however: between 1902, when a basement was excavated under the church and a furnace installed, and 1955, when the

Christ Church has an unusual design, with its aisles housed under two low-sloped roofs. The bell tower was later enclosed to prevent rain and melting snow from seeping into the church. (Saskatchewan Archives Board R-A 7390)

basement was filled in to stabilize the building.

Such quirky milestones, along with the sounds and smells, contributed to the unique personality of Christ Anglican Church. In the beginning, however, there was only the Canadian Pacific Railway. The section foreman and his wife also arrived in 1882 and, in the section house, were soon hosting Anglican services conducted by Rev. J. P. Sargent, a travelling missionary whose name appears in the early accounts of many Anglican churches along the CPR main line.

A history compiled by an early member of the congregation tells of some parishioners driving twelve miles (20 km) by horse and buggy to attend these Anglican services, a fund for construction of a church being started in 1889, and two parishioners hauling stones from the surrounding fields in readiness for the building of the church in 1891.

But nothing is recorded of the person who designed the 35-by-45-foot (11 m × 14 m) church with arches that are pointed in the Gothic style over the entrance, chancel, west window, and side windows, but rounded in the Romanesque style at the end of the chancel. Neither is anything known of the man who laid the fieldstones in a random rubble style and outlined all the arches with yellow brick.

In a community of only fifty adults, Christ Anglican Church was impressive. Inside, as described by a correspondent for *The Church Messenger* on the occasion of the November 22, 1891 consecration by Bishop Anson, was a different story: "As it is a rule never to consecrate a church in debt, your readers can imagine better than I can describe the efforts the committee have had to put forth in capturing enough cash to pay off the many various accounts. Much more, however, must be done to make the interior complete; the rough stone walls have a cheerless and unfinished appearance, and have yet to be plastered and there is a good deal of carpenter work to do. Organ and pulpit and many other necessary articles have to be obtained. . . ."

The finishing touches were gradual: plaster three years later; an oak altar, reredos, pews and organ, and a small house next door for the first resident priest six years later; and a brass bell "of outstanding tone" at the same time as the new basement and furnace.

Eventually, structural problems along the north side were noted and then addressed by the addition of three buttresses. But these began sinking, pulling the wall with them. In 1955, therefore, two buttresses were removed and the basement was filled in. Because the open cupola was collecting snow in winter and birds in summer, it was enclosed at the same time, and drilled with the design of the cross, rather like a pie cupboard.

As in all small churches in rural Saskatchewan, much of this work was paid for by Women's Auxiliary projects. But, after eighty years of dedicated service by successive generations of women, only four members remained, and they decided they could no longer carry on. This signalled the beginning of the end. The congregation of Christ Anglican Church

closed its doors in 1982.

The church, now owned by the Town of Wapella, was designated a municipal heritage property in 1990. A group of volunteers, like the erstwhile Women's Auxiliary, maintain it through fundraising projects and the sweat of their brows. By replacing the cedar roof, for example, they stopped the leaks that have streaked the plaster walls, but they fret about the cost of replacing the rotting window frames around the red, blue, and yellow glass that still casts a warm glow on the carved oak furnishings below.

"I guess we will just have to frame one window at a time," says Norma Crossman, who volunteered because she and four others "just like the church and got together to try and fix it up. We don't have a name. We just do it."

Praise the Lord. ❧

MIDDLE LEFT: One of the side windows displays an attractive mix of coloured glass.

The popular pointed Gothic-style arch is used in the apse and east stained-glass windows of Christ Church, seen here from inside. The use of the Gothic arch is continued inside the church as well as for the windows and door.

Our Lady of Assumption (Kaposvar) Roman Catholic Church

NEAR ESTERHAZY

Looming darkly over farm fields rolling down to distant Esterhazy, the stone church of Kaposvar recalls two romantic architectural styles – Gothic and medieval – and promises tales of mystery and love. That promise is fulfilled. The history of Our Lady of Assumption Roman Catholic Church, part of the Kaposvar Historic Site, begins with a man whose identity remains controversial, and continues with the same love that inspired its builders. ❦ First the romance. According to the biography "The Mysterious Count Esterhazy" by G. V. Dojcsak, John Packh was born in Hungary in 1831, the son of an architect and a woman who, it was rumoured, had been impregnated by Nicholas Esterhazy, a member of Hungary's most prominent and wealthy family. When John was eight, his father was murdered

The roof extension to the front of the church created a large gable, which was parged with concrete.

ended in the British West Indies, where he "absconded" and eloped with the twenty-two-year-old daughter of a British officer.

He returned to Hungary and, as he later wrote, assumed his "rightful name, Paul O. d'Esterhazy, by incontroversial proof of the legality of my claim and of inviolable birth right." Leaving John Packh behind, he arrived in the United States in 1868. In 1885, after a variety of enterprises and, finally, contact with Canada's Agriculture department and the Canadian Pacific Railway, he and a Hungarian agriculture expert visited Manitoba and the Qu'Appelle Valley in the North-West Territories to determine their suitability for agricultural colonies. A year later, a Hungarian settlement was established forty kilometres north of Whitewood.

According to a report by "Count d'Esterhazy," the CPR afforded free transportation from Toronto to Winnipeg to fifty Hungarian families from the New York and Pennsylvania areas, and $25,000 was advanced by Sir George Stephen of the CPR to buy

and his mother was briefly imprisoned for complicity in the crime.

John eventually joined the Hungarian army and was quickly promoted, again prompting rumours of his illicit birth. Exiled as a revolutionary, he was granted asylum in Britain, where he joined the army. His military adventures

animals, implements and the lumber to build houses. Settling on land made available by the CPR, the colony was registered as Esterhaz.

About two-thirds of the homesteaders soon left Esterhaz but, in 1888, more Hungarian families arrived. A year later, a Department of Immigration inspector described the settlement as "flourishing," but the Count "departed for the United States 'under a cloud.'" He died in New York in 1912.

Meanwhile, a new post office registered as Kaposvar (a centre of Esterhazy estates in Hungary) was established in the area in 1890 and, when a CPR branch line arrived in the district in 1902, the village of Esterhazy was soon incorporated five kilometres north of the Kaposvar post office.

Before the arrival of the Hungarians, however, Father Jules Decorby had been conducting mass in what was to become the parish of Our Lady of Assumption. When Archbishop Taché of St. Boniface read about the Hungarian arrivals, he sent out Father Page to hold mass and, eventually, to build a log church on seven acres of donated land. *Kaposvar: A Count's Colony 1886–1986* reports that a subsequent priest, Father Woodcutter, had a ten-room rectory built of stone in 1901–03. When the next priest, Father Pirot, arrived, he decided the congregation needed a larger church as well so, in 1906, he returned to his native Belgium to obtain plans. He returned to Kaposvar with the stonemasons too: his brothers Alphone and Camille and his brother-in-law, Octave Wuilleaume.

Parishioners hauled 1,600 loads of stone by sleigh in preparation for the building of the church in the summer of 1907. It was completed and dedicated by the Archbishop of St Boniface in 1908.

The size, bulk, buttresses and the small openings in the shorter tower suggest a medieval influence on its design, while the pointed arches relate to the Gothic style. The stonework resembles that of the rectory: multi-coloured and multisize stones laid in a random rubble style. Each stone was originally outlined with white.

Changes have occurred since construction, however.

The two-storey rectory was constructed in 1901–03, several years before the church.

By 1936, the roof between the towers had been extended forward, and while the new gabled wall still contained a niche for the sculpted Virgin Mary, it was faced with concrete. Concrete was also applied to the stonework between the windows along the side walls.

The interior has also changed. In the 1940s, for example, the ceiling was painted with *trompe l'oeil* panels framing religious symbols, and in the 1970s, storms destroyed all the stained-glass windows in the nave.

Attendance is different too. Although weddings and funerals are held, regular mass is not. Still, the annual August pilgrimage to the Shrine of Our Lady of Lourdes continues, the church and rectory are maintained and open to visitors every summer, and former parishioners remain steadfast in their love for the site. "The statues look so friendly," says Elizabeth Tomaluck, adding, "My grandmother – she came from Pittsburgh with my grandfather in 1888 – bought The Little Child of Prague. She prayed to it. And the men in the choir had such loud, strong voices. Those Hungarians sing so beautifully. The church gave you peace, contentment.

"It still does." ❧

OPPOSITE: One of Saskatchewan's oldest stone places of worship, St. John's Anglican Church was completed in 1885, the same year that Canadians fought one another on the battlegrounds only 265 kilometres northwest of Fort Qu'Appelle.

St. John the Evangelist Anglican Church

FORT QU'APPELLE

Tucked into a corner off a shady street in Fort Qu'Appelle, the humble tranquility of the small fieldstone St. John the Evangelist Church belies a history that is as eventful as any in the province. ❧ Completed in 1885, just months after the North-West Rebellion ended, St. John's records date to 1822, when Hudson's Bay Company chaplain John West conducted services and administered the sacraments during his three-week visit to the Qu'Appelle Valley, then a part of what was known as Rupert's Land and owned by the Hudson's Bay Company. On his return to the Red River area in what is now Manitoba, Rev. John West established a school to train young Aboriginal men for missionary work. ❧ One of the first graduates of this school, Charles Pratt, was given the task of building a mission

The addition of a corner tower greatly enhanced the prominence of St. John's Church in the community.

and a hymn was sung in the Cree language.

In 1859, however, Rev. Settee terminated the mission due to opposition from the Indians who feared that bison herds would be driven away by settlement of the area.

By 1864, the Hudson's Bay Company had moved its trading post from near what is now Qu'Appelle to the present site of Fort Qu'Appelle, and officers of the company were occasionally reading the scriptures to Church of England settlers drawn to the area. By 1883, services were being held in the town hall and, a year later, the parish was named St. John the Evangelist. The first wardens were appointed in 1884 as well, one of whom was Captain John French, who was killed at Batoche during the North-West Rebellion the following year.

Most Rev. Adelbert Anson, first Bishop of the Qu'Appelle Diocese, consecrated the fieldstone St. John the Evangelist Church on December 27, 1885, setting it apart "from all common and profane uses." Four days later, *The Vidette* described both the service and the

between Echo and Mission lakes, a site decided upon by Rev. Charles Hillyer who, in 1852 and '54, had spent time in the valley attempting to win souls among the Saulteaux and Cree Indians. These early "Church of England" activities are further described in the St. John's *Jubilee Memento* booklet, which quotes a passage from a book by "a party of surveyors [who] visited the western prairies":

The Qu'Appelle Mission is situated between the second and third Fishing Lakes; it was established in 1858. For some time past, however, Charles Pratt, the catechist, has resided where the mission is situated, and has constructed a comfortable log house. The Rev. James Settee, the missionary, a native of Swampy Cree origin, occupied Pratt's house; the Rev. Mr. Settee read the prayers in English with great ease and correctness; he preached in Ojibway,

church. The interior plastered walls, it reported, were a "delicate pinkish tint," the wainscoting "stained a dark oak hue," and the ceiling "varnished pine stained oak." The masonry and plastering had been carried out by "Messers Gibson and Turner." Unfortunately, "the tower and steeple over the northwest door were not built owning to the lateness of the season." Subsequent records indicate that the square stone tower was added in 1902 and the stone vestry in 1904.

The tower stonework is similar to that of the original, random-rubble style of the body, and all the Gothic-style windows and doors are outlined with buff-coloured brick. Similar bricks were used for the quoins at the corners of the original structure, while the tower has stone buttresses at the first-storey corners, and larger stones at the second-storey corners.

According to *Jubilee Memento,* a "wooden contraption" replaced the hip roof of the tower in 1904 to enhance the sound of the bell. According to Derek Harrison, church organist since the 1950s, the contraption blew off in 1957, and was replaced by a fieldstone extension, "built by the grandson of the man who built the original church and tower."

The interior, with its east-facing chancel separated from the nave by a pointed arch and a brass chancel rail, is similar to many small Anglican churches in the province, but is notable for the ceiling beams arching across the width and terminating in pendant finials. Everything within it has been donated in memory of deceased clergy or members of the congregation, from the white altar frontal handmade in England in the 1890s, to the pews made locally in 1950, and

the stained glass windows that first date to 1946.

The written history of St. John's is as colourful as the windows. A description of rectors from 1885 to 1933, for example, tells of one who "thought the Anglican Church was the greatest invention since altar bread," and another "who is perhaps better remembered for the freedom of expression of his many children." Even the official *Jubilee Memento* includes précis of various rectors, such as one who "got married and preached much better sermons ever after," and another whose "horses will be remembered much longer than his sermons."

Regular Sunday sermons at St. John the Evangelist, memorable or not, continue today. ❧

The bell tower on St. John's Church, constructed in 1902, was originally topped with a low-hipped roof. (Saskatchewan Archives Board R-B 1813)

MIDDLE LEFT: The main stained glass window at St. John's Church includes scenes from the community's past.

OPPOSITE: St. Paul's Church, the workmanship of local stonemasons Charlie Parker and his son Harold, is almost identical to that of St. David's Anglican Church in Maryfield, also built by the Parkers.

St. Paul's Anglican Church

NEAR LANGBANK

While emotional and intellectual impulses can now be tracked to their origins in the human brain, creativity remains a mystery: the process, for example, that resulted in the design of St. Paul's Anglican Church two kilometres south of Langbank. ❧ This fieldstone sanctuary escapes – but just barely – the descriptive word "quaint" only because of its imposing Norman-style tower complete with crenellation. Built by a congregation rendered penniless by the Great Depression of the 1930s, its size and materials were dictated by their reduced circumstances, but why its unique style? Why the tiny cave-like apse and a nave with windows deep-set into the exterior stone walls like a fisherman's cottage in Scotland's Hebridean Islands? ❧ The answers lie buried behind the church, in the gravevsite

The interior of St. Paul's Church displays the white-plastered stone walls and the warmth of a wooden open-beam ceiling.

The parish history goes on to describe the first day of June that year, when eleven teams of horses hauled 180 loads of stones and 30 loads of gravel to a one-acre site donated by another member of the building committee. It was also noted that "Ladies of the congregation assisted the men in throwing off the stone from the wagons . . ."

Archbishop Knowles laid St. Paul's cornerstone in mid-June and, despite the lack of doors and windows, the first service was held in mid-August. The opening service was held in mid-September, with the combined choir of the Anglican churches at Wawota and Cannington Manor. "The Church was packed, 125 people present," continues the history, to which Earl Debenham of Kennedy now adds dubiously, "If they weren't big people." Earl attended that 1938 service, but he was six at the time. As one of today's three remaining members of the congregation – his wife and brother are the other two – he suspects exaggeration. "Thirty-five was the usual attendance and that's about right for comfort."

of one of its builders, Charles J. Parker, who died in 1955 at the age of eighty-one. Described by his gravestone as "A Man of Faith Who Laboured With Stone," Charlie had sharpened his masonry skills with training in the United States, but he was first taught the trade by his mother's brothers in Bobcaygeon, Ontario. His maternal family had come there from Scotland, where the men had learned stonemasonry. Adding to the appeal of St. Paul's, therefore, is speculation that its style is due to the atavistic impulse, that it derived from the land of its designers' forefathers.

Without question, its design was also due to practicality. When the Mission of Langbank's building committee, which included Charlie and his stonemason son, Harold, held a meeting in March 1938, the members decided it was possible to build a stone church "if all the work was voluntary, as at the time we had absolutely no funds available."

This comfort was only possible from Easter to Thanksgiving. As a youth, says Earl, his job was to light and tend the little wood-burning stove a couple of days before the first service of the year: "Once those stones get cold, it's hard to warm them."

Those stones, covered with a lime wash, formed the interior walls as well. The open ceiling was lined with unvarnished tongue-and-groove fir. The Sherlock-Manning pump organ was donated, as were two coal-oil lamps. Twelve old pews were bought for $20 from St. Luke's Church in Broadview, and were painted by the women of the congregation. The church history notes they "will be used for a time." But, seventy years later, nothing has changed.

The exception to this charming and authentic rusticity is the natural fieldstone arch over the small blue apse, the latter illuminated by a little window with a pale, stained-glass cross. The stones in the slightly pointed arch were chosen, cut, and laid as if for a bishop's cathedral.

Strangely enough, the master craftsmanship of the arch is not as evident in the walls. The tower features quoins of mostly limestone with two massive pink sandstones, as well as a large limestone cross above the door, but all are roughly shaped and placed with little apparent regard for order. The remaining stones are uncut and laid in a random-rubble style, and the door and windows are rectangular in shape.

Interestingly, the Parkers built St. David Anglican Church in Maryfield a year later and, at first glance, the two churches appear identical. But they're not: although St. David's shape is similar and its tower crenellation is also of concrete, its proportions are more pleasing; its door and windows have pointed arches; and its stonework, including the cross above the entrance, is more finely wrought than at St. Paul's.

Not that anyone notices or cares. Although guarded by three hundred evergreens planted in 1940, and modestly set back from a busy highway, St. Paul's draws dozens of visitors through its unlocked door every year. All are awed by its simple beauty. And

more: "Comfort is here" one visitor wrote in the summer of 2006.

That same summer, just before the bride joined her groom at the home-made altar, a mouse ran across the aisle. "A church mouse," the mother-of-the-bride wrote in her thank-you note to the Debenhams. "It was perfect." ❧

ABOVE: The small half-round apse with its conical roof is an unusual design feature for Saskatchewan churches.

BELOW: Charles and Rebecca Parker both died in 1955, and are buried in St. Paul's Cemetery. Their epitaphs read: "Charles: A Man of Faith Who Labored With Stone" and "Rebecca: Distinguished for Her Kindness to All Living Creatures."

OPPOSITE: St. Lucy's Anglican Church
is one of the smallest stone churches
in Saskatchewan, but stands majestically
on a corner intersection in the village
of Dilke, proudly proclaiming its
ecclesiastical function.

St. Lucy's Anglican Church

DILKE

It's a tiny perfect church with a history to match. ❧ For example, St. Lucy's Anglican Church at Dilke was named for the Christian martyr St. Lucy, but it was also named for Lucy Sawbridge, the young wife of the first parish priest. She died before she could join her husband in Canada. ❧ The lectern was made, allegedly with jackknives, by members of the unit led by a parishioner who was killed during the First World War. ❧ But it's not all tragedy. There's the story of the church's first bride, who arrived in the rain, discovered she was locked out, and entered through a window – to the huge amusement of those small boys who always seem to be present on such occasions. ❧ As with most early churches in Saskatchewan, St. Lucy's history begins with a devotional need that was met with services in the settlers'

The projecting shoulders at the base of the roofline give this building the appearance of being larger than it actually is.

site of Dilke about the time the Canadian Pacific Railway laid tracks through the area in 1911. A school was built the same year, and in 1912, a young Anglican priest from Norwich, England, Rev. J. E. Sawbridge, arrived to conduct services in that school.

When his wife died soon after, he immediately left for England to care for their twin boys, but promised to raise money to help build a church for the congregation and the area that had so impressed him. "In due time," states *Ploughshares and Prairie Trails: Dilke & District,* "money began to arrive from England, and on August 14, 1914 the cornerstone was laid . . ."

The cornerstone and others were picked from parishioners' fields, with many hauled by a pair of oxen who pulled their wagon to and from the church without a driver but expected – and received – right of way. They were remembered as "road hogs."

The original design for the church was drawn by A. J. Rowley, a Regina-based architect at the time and

homes. In the Dilke district, these settlers were part of the province's second wave of immigration, and they clustered around the surveyed

responsible for the fieldstone Anglican church at Heward as well. His plan was modified and reduced in size by J. Stewart Houston, a Tyvan homesteader who was related to a Dilke settler and had taken drafting during a university agriculture course.

The obvious influence on this plan was the Gothic revival style, as evidenced by the pointed arch of the door and six windows, as well as the gabled ends with shoulders, a common feature of late Gothic revival churches in England. And it is this architectural style, reminiscent of the great cathedrals of England and France, combined with the simplicity, diminutive size and common fieldstone that give St. Lucy's Church such charm.

The stonemason was Baptist lay reader Ben Brewer, who had arrived in Dilke from England in 1912 to further his church's cause. A builder by trade, he laid St. Lucy's shaped stones in courses that remain cohesive today, and outlined the door and windows with concrete blocks that have not moved an inch.

Little has changed inside either. Thirty-seven mismatched wooden chairs are ranged before a wood chancel rail pierced by Tudor-arched openings. A potbelly Blazer stove stands in one corner, a Thomas pump organ in another. Above the altar is a relief painting of Mary and the Christ child. It was donated by the women and children of St. Margaret's Church in Norwich when they "adopted" St. Lucy's.

Research in the 1970s revealed a list of those St. Margaret's contributors and, after contact with No. 10 Downing Street, confirmed that one of the children on the list, Harold Wilson, eventually became prime minister of England.

By the 1970s, St. Lucy's had been closed as a church for about twenty years and was maintained as a symbol of the faith that sustained the first settlers in the district, not only Anglicans but also those of other denominations. Ecumenism is not a new concept in rural Saskatchewan. A Baptist constructed St. Lucy's, a United Church organist played for

services, and a Roman Catholic neighbour safeguards it today.

But one woman whose grandparents were Dilke homesteaders, whose name appears on St. Lucy's "Font Roll of Little Helpers" and who decorates the deep window wells for the annual Harvest Thanksgiving service, says, "After my generation – we're all over fifty – I'm afraid St. Lucy's will be forgotten."

Then, sitting at the Thomas pump organ, she plays the hymn sung at every Harvest Thanksgiving, "For Beauty of Prairies." The stones of St. Lucy's are a hymn to that beauty as well. And they will endure. ✤

A small recessed cross was cast into the concrete keystone over the door

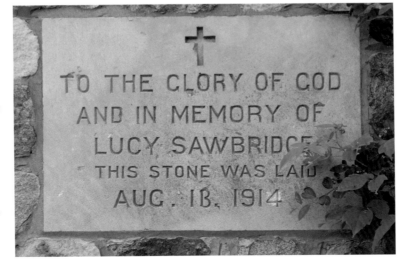

The datestone at St. Lucy's Anglican Church, Dilke. Was the original ceremony slated for August 11th or 13th changed to August 18, or did the manufacturer carve the wrong date, then make a correction?

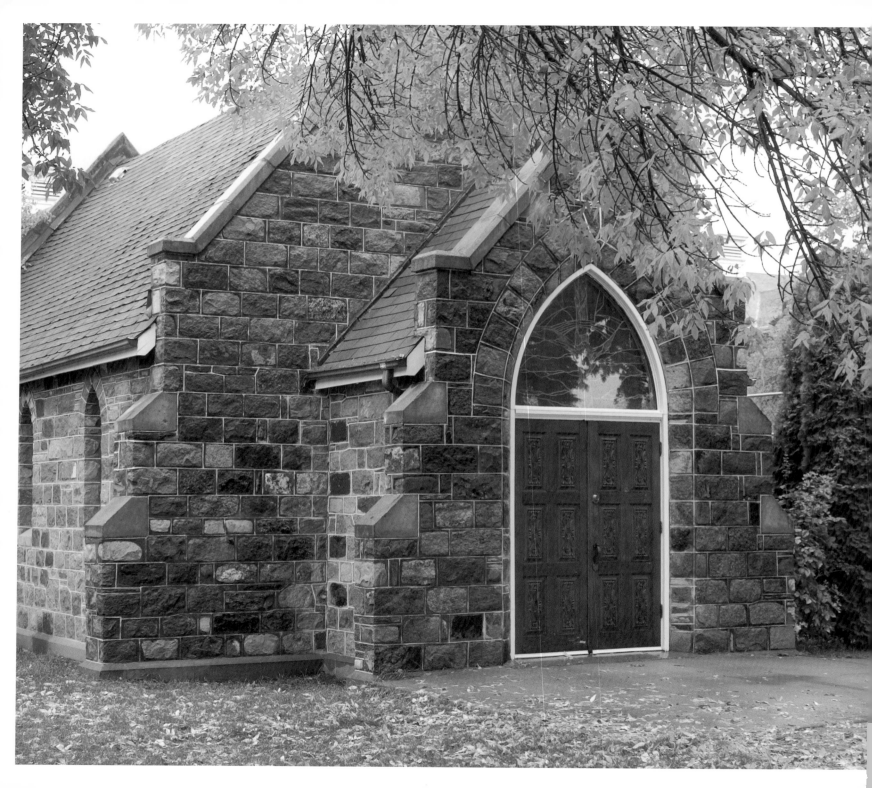

OPPOSITE: The stepped buttress-like ends of the Saskatchewan Hospital Chapel suggest a design based upon a more substantial church. As with the church at Dilke, it includes projecting shoulders at the base of the gable rooflines.

Saskatchewan Hospital Chapel

NORTH BATTLEFORD

The diminutive perfection of the chapel at the Saskatchewan Hospital in North Battleford has charmed visitors ever since it was completed in 1942. The Gothic-style windows and the steeply gabled ends, each with parapets, buttress-like sides and even a lancet window, are reminiscent of the village churches of thirteenth-century England, while the stones were obviously chosen, cut and placed with the hands of a craftsman and the eye of an artist. ❧ This perfection, however, is suffused with tragedy. ❧ The Hospital for the Insane in North Battleford was designed by the Regina architectural firm Storey and Van Egmond, and was built of brick on 2,250 acres of land overlooking the North Saskatchewan River. It received its first patients in 1914. ❧ In May 1940, Saskatoon architect E. J. Gilbert was commissioned to

The Gothic influence is clearly evident in the pointed arches used for both the door and windows of this small building.

design a mortuary chapel to be squeezed into a rear corner of the main building and connected to it by a tunnel. According to a 1960s report by Dr. Maurice Demay, superintendent of what was then known as the Saskatchewan Hospital, North Battleford, the plans for the chapel called for fieldstone walls with concrete "trim," "oaken front doors with trefoil apertures," and high over the altar, a rose window. Because it reflected such cathedrals as Rheims and Canterbury, he wrote, "Little wonder that the general exterior of this little chapel, steeped in the classics, should attract such a moving and pleasing interest." It was built to accommodate forty-four, but could seat up to sixty within its 600 square feet (55 m²), Dr. Demay continued.

While going on to detail "its more mundane aspects," such as central steam heat and a washroom beside the main entrance, he did not mention the morgue in the basement. Perhaps because, by the 1960s, burials no longer took place in the cemeteries located on the hospital grounds, Dr. Demay stressed its use as an interdenominational place of worship: "Its meaning must be found in the very roots of human nature which calls for the dignity of man both in life and in death. Over and beyond the value of things material are to be reckoned the superior and everlasting spiritual values. It is a place where man may quietly turn to his God and commune with him in silent prayer and meditation."

Was the peace that comes with silent prayer and meditation ever attained by Emil Schoen? He was the man who so carefully chose the building stones from those gathered from the hospital farm lands by other patients and placed in piles for his inspection; the man who so precisely shaped these stones for laying in the ashlar style, the best grade of stonemasonry.

His portrait, a large, black-and-white photograph framed in an oak oval, labelled with a brass plaque, and hung in the chapel, does not show a man at peace with either himself or God.

Emil was born in Germany in 1886 and arrived with his wife in Saskatoon in 1913. He was admitted to the Saskatchewan Mental Hospital, North Battleford in 1921, a thirty-five-year-old father of four. He remained a patient at this hospital until he died on March 28, 1970, three weeks after the amputation of his gangrenous right leg at the North Battleford Union Hospital. He was eighty-three.

Emil's wife had told hospital staff that he was a bricklayer by trade, and had always been busy and hardworking. This aspect of his life never changed. Not only did he carry out most of the two-year construction of the chapel, he was responsible for almost all the stonework at the hospital, including bridges, retaining walls and gate pillars.

"He liked to work by himself, and he didn't talk to many people . . . ," recalled one of the hospital's paid plasterers, quoted in a 1971 newspaper article. "We never had to worry about his end of the

job. Emil understood the building business. Often if he saw you working on something he would finish what he was doing at the time, then come and ask if he could help you."

Today, worshipers attending the weekly service at the Saskatchewan Hospital Chapel, North Battleford may note the tribute to Emil and also one of the wall-hangings: "And God looked at what He had made and it was very good. Genesis." Whether Emil ever saw the tribute or believed these words is unknown. But it is comforting to know that he was buried from the chapel, and the evidence of his artistic soul remains. ⚘

The regular coursing of the stonework and the variety of stone colours well complement the green roof on the chapel.

The stone bridge crossing a very small creek on the hospital grounds is another example of stonemason Emil Schoen's high-quality craftsmanship.

Fairview Methodist Church

NEAR DAVIN

Fairview Methodist Church is best discovered on a cold, snow-laden day. Bravely trimmed with red, and facing down all that the northern plains can inflict, it stands on the highest point of the rolling prairie north of Davin, its simple, wind-whipped countenance a symbol of the men and women who built it. Indeed, it could be a symbol of the men and women who built the province of Saskatchewan. In summer, the grasses that first covered this landmark hill are cut for hay by Richard Shaw, grandson of Levi Shaw, one of Fairview's founding members. Richard farms from Levi's home quarter, just down the road from the church. Levi, the son of English-born Ontario settlers, arrived in the North-West Territories in 1882, walked from Regina with a shovel to check the soil at Davin – or so

Situated on a height of land on the vast open prairie near Regina, this church has always been difficult to access during the winter months.

family lore has it – and applied for a homestead. His descendants honour his claim of being the first settler in the district.

According to another of Levi's grandsons, Jim Shaw, the first Fairview Methodist Church was a frame building constructed on the same rise of land seven years after Levi arrived. Jim says the stone church was built to replace the frame church after it burned down in a prairie fire on April 14, 1902. But a June 7, 1902 entry in the "Minutes of Meetings of The Board of Trustees of Fairview

Methodist Church and Cemetery" states, "Minutes of meeting held in Fairview Church to see about building a new church on motion of William Brown, L. Shaw . . ."

The reason for building a new church may remain a mystery, but the methodical progress toward completion of it is clearly outlined in subsequent minutes. At the June meeting, for example, it was "moved that we build a stone church size 30 × 40 [9 × 12 m]," and that the district be canvassed for funds. Two months later, eight men,

including Levi, promised to draw one cord of stone each.

By March 1903, the proposed size of the church had been reduced to "26 × 40 outside [8 × 12 m]," architect Alexander Malcolm Fraser of Indian Head was scheduled to provide plans and specifications, and a bee was to be arranged to draw sand. By July, the architect and his plans had been approved, James W. Smith had been hired to carry out the masonry for $350, and Pilot Butte Brick Company had been asked to supply 1,400 bricks.

The architect's plans and specifications, which are kept by Richard, call for "Black mortar with a White line in block style or rustic pattern as per wishes of the inspector . . . so that the White Painting lines, Black mortar and natural stone will form a good contrast." Of these specifications, only the natural stone remain; if black mortar and white lines ever existed, they have faded, allowing the soft greys, blues, pinks, and reds to warm the sky on a snow-chilled day or become one with the land on a late autumn afternoon.

The cornerstones are large and native to the area, but the largest of the other stones is not more than twenty centimetres square. Near the roof line the stones are closer to the fist-size rocks that Richard says continue to rise to the surface long after Levi picked the first of them. The only evidence that the goal when laying these stones was more than durability and straight walls – that stonemason Smith had an artistic eye – is the burgundy keystone in the Gothic-styled entrance arch. And perhaps it was this stone that prompted the deeper shade of burgundy on the door, concrete sills, wrap-around eaves and slightly flared gable ends. Or perhaps, as Jim jokes, burgundy was chosen because "it was left-over barn paint."

Originally, the woodwork in the front gable was more elaborate, with spandrels, drop pendants and more cutouts, but the years have taken their toll, leaving only three bars radiating up from the cross-piece. Time has been unkind to the windows as well. When installed, they were as the architect directed: "All the centre lights to be filled with red muffled glass and all side lights with blue of same quality." Inside, the embossed metal ceiling is intact but peeling. The walls are stained and the white paint on the balusters, railing and newel posts outlining the front platform is becoming faint. The pump organ and six ornate chairs on the platform were stolen in the 1970s.

The congregation of Fairview Methodist Church became part of the United Church of Canada in 1925, and the last service was held in the early 1960s. Still, it was standing room only – there never were pews, and all the chairs are gone – at the celebration of the hundred years since the cornerstone was laid August 18, 1903. Of the more than seventy celebrants, many were descendants of the founding members, some still farming their ancestors' homesteads. Those ancestors lie in the cemetery behind the church. The Shaw brothers care for the cemetery too.

"It's just the way you do things," says Jim. ❧

The roofline of the church is slightly flared at its base, while decorative timbers are incorporated into the top of the gable.

The stones for the window and door arches have been carefully selected to form a self-supporting structure, while larger stones, including the datestone, have been incorporated into the corners for greater strength.

Sacred Heart
Roman Catholic Church

LEBRET

A s if its unexpected beauty were not enough, the Qu'Appelle Valley has always been a land of legend as well. The origin of its very name, for example, is explained by several different tales, and one story of Lebret at the east end of Mission Lake tells of its accidental founding by a supposedly bumbling Bishop Alexandre Taché. ❧ But it was no accident. According to the 1929 "Codex Historicus of the Qu'Appelle Mission," Bishop Taché, Oblate of Mary Immaculate (O.M.I.), St. Boniface, chose to camp at the present site of Lebret in August 1864 on his way to Ile-a-la-Crosse. As a result of his encounter with the Métis Catholics of the area, three Métis men travelled to Red River to ask for a resident priest, and in October 1865, the French-speaking Oblates sent Bishop Taché back

The spire, clad in sheet metal, also houses the bell and significantly increases the visibility of the church from afar.

Fort Qu'Appelle and witnessing the traffic in liquor, he determined to locate this mission eight kilometres east, at the site of his camp a year previous. He named it St. Florent after Rev. Florent Vandenbergh, o.m.i., at Ile-a-la-Crosse.

Rev. J. N. Ritchot of St. Boniface, assisted by local Métis, built a poplar-log chapel-residence with a thatched roof in 1866, and in 1868, the first resident priest, Rev. Jules Decorby, o.m.i., built a bigger church-residence, which burned down the next year. A new church and separate residence were built in 1870, the church facing Mission Lake for the convenience of parishioners arriving by canoe. Rev. Louis Lebret, o.m.i., arrived in 1884, and requested the name of the parish be changed to *Sacré Coeur de Jesus.* He also applied to have the postal address given the same name. While the former was granted, the latter became Lebret instead.

By early 1920, the congregation had increased to 171 families and the particulars of a proposed new church were being discussed. At one meeting, for example, it was decided that

to the valley to judge the feasibility of this proposal.

Inspired by the valley's beauty, Taché immediately decided to establish a mission but, after staying overnight at

"all those who work for a salary and are a head of a family will give $1 a month" toward the building of this church, while a later meeting decided that the church, to be built on the site of the one that had burned down, would face the "*montagne*" instead of the lake.

The church was designed by Brother Jean-Théodore de Byl, o.m.i., who was born in Holland and trained as an architect in Germany and Holland. After making his perpetual vows in Manitoba in 1894, he served in parishes across Saskatchewan, Manitoba and western Ontario. He designed a number of schools, churches and residences, at least five of which are in Saskatchewan: Indian Residential School, Marieval (1897); Church of the Assumption, Holdfast (1922); St. Joseph's Church, Marcelin (1923); Sacred Heart Church, Lebret (1925); and probably his final design, Sacred Heart Scholasticate on Mission Lake's south shore, completed in 1927, less than a year after his death.

Brother de Byl's design for Sacred Heart Church, which is almost identical to Holdfast's church, is reminiscent of traditional Roman Catholic churches in Quebec, combining elements of Gothic, Romanesque, and classical architecture. Its spire and rose windows, for example, are commonly associated with Gothic revival but, instead of Gothic-style pointed arches, the doors and windows are round-arched in the Romanesque style. The Quebec similarities are apparent in the use of fieldstone as the main building material, with stone trim and a metal-clad belfry featuring a column-supported pediment.

Inside, the barrel-vaulted ceilings of the nave and transept intersect to create a graceful groin vault. Deep, dentiled cornices, supported by Corinthian columns, frame the coffered ceiling above the side aisles. Suffusing the whole is light through three tall windows on each side, one at each end of the transept and two lunettes above the apse.

While the interior is a graceful paean to God's glory – as well as a capacious space for five hundred – Sacred Heart also attests to the willingness of God's people to

work towards that glory. For years, for example, parishioners hauled stones from their fields every time they came to town, eventually creating cords that lined the site. "And, during construction, Joe Desjarlais carried the big stones all by himself. He was considered the strongest man in the valley," says eighty-something Jimmy LaRocque, grandson of respected Métis leader John Antoine LaRocque. "Old Delorme was our only stonemason. He could split stones like that . . ." Jimmy continues, slicing the air with his hands.

Moses Delorme worked under the supervision of William Dunnett, who trained as a stonemason in Edinburgh, Scotland, and immigrated to Winnipeg in 1911. William, who also worked on buildings such as Toronto's Royal York Hotel and Winnipeg's Fort Garry Hotel, was hired by the Oblates in St. Boniface.

The Tyndall stone for the corners, string courses and surrounds of the door and windows of the primary façade came from Manitoba. The remainder of the corners

The Stations of the Cross lead to a chapel on the north slope of the Qu'Appelle Valley opposite Sacred Heart Roman Catholic Church, Lebret.

and window surrounds are of fieldstone, while the second-storey walls behind the transept are of galvanized iron, the same as the roof, belfry, and parapets.

On completion of the fieldstone walls, William returned to Winnipeg. As he was boarding the train, a church representative shook his hand and said, "You have built a monument of the future."

Or maybe he didn't. Maybe the story of the Church of the Sacred Heart of Jesus is just another Qu'Appelle Valley legend. According to the records, the church was completed in 1925 (MCMXXV) but, etched over a fossil in the datestone, is the mythical number MXMXXV. ❧

St. Mary the Virgin Anglican Church

WHITEWOOD

The Canadian Pacific Railway reached the Whitewood area in 1882, and the Anglicans weren't far behind. ❧ Members of St. Mary the Virgin Anglican Church, in fact, have always been proud to tell of the first Anglican service in Whitewood, conducted by a licensed layreader, on July 11, 1883. Two months later, Rev. Canon W. H. Cooper celebrated communion in a tent with twelve communicants. Services continued in the waiting room of the CPR station until 1885, when a small wooden church named St. Mary's was built. This is when the memorial donations, which have continued ever since, began. One of the most storied of these was a stained-glass window that languished in storage for a year because the vestry was to pay its freight and customs duty but couldn't come up with the money. ❧ Another

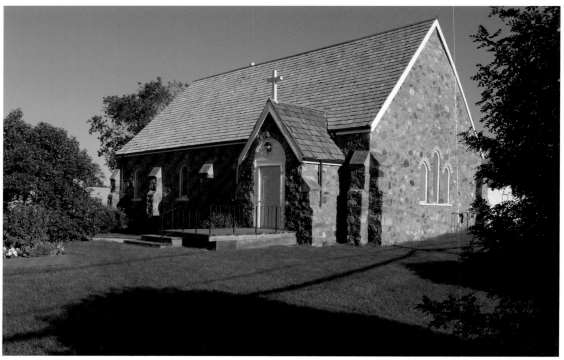

The view of St. Mary's from the northwest provides a very different perspective on this church. The buttresses are also visible, particularly at the corners.

example of the financial straits of parishioners in the late 1800s – still adapting to the agricultural methods demanded by their adopted land, most homesteaders in the District of Assiniboia were struggling at that time – was the foundation of the new church: it was laid in 1898 but, due to lack of funds, the building was not started until 1902.

When construction of the church began, it reflected yet another characteristic of the late 1800s in Whitewood.

Although a predominantly Anglo-Saxon community itself, it was surrounded by colonies established by ethnically diverse groups – French to the south, Finns to the northeast, and Scots, Hungarians and Swedes to the north – so it was not surprising the stonemason responsible for St. Mary the Virgin was Eric Berg, a Lutheran who had learned his craft in Sweden and arrived as a homesteader in the New Stockholm District in 1887.

"Fields of White" a centennial history of the church (1883–1983) tells of the fieldstones for the church being drawn from surrounding farms to the site of the new church by horse and wagon. Limestone was quarried and reduced to lime on a parishioner's farm. The stones, none of them remarkably large, were laid in the random-rubble building style. Their soft colours varied from tan through gold to a blue-grey and, occasionally, a near burgundy. Pale stone wedges were used to outline the arches of the side windows and main entrance, with Tyndall stone over the three arched windows at the rear. The pointed arch of the windows and the buttressed corners and side walls are reminiscent of Gothic architecture.

Bishop Grisdale – the second bishop of the Diocese of Qu'Appelle, which was created in 1883 and followed the boundaries of the civil District of Assiniboia – consecrated the pretty St. Mary the Virgin Anglican Church in July 1902.

The vestry, its stones and mortar indistinguishable from

the body of the church, was added near the traditional east-facing chancel and consecrated in 1913. Above the vestry is a shingled bell tower, and the bell within it "has a sweet sound, not tinny at all," says parishioner Doreen Westcott, whose Anglican ancestors arrived in the Whitewood district in 1885.

In the years since the vestry was built, only the roof has changed: the small triangular dormers that originally ranged across each side are gone. Inside, the original plastered walls with varnished cedar wainscoting have been covered with new material, but the ceiling is still varnished tongue-and-groove cedar decoratively laid in four-foot (1.2 m) squares that meet at the corners with bull's-eyes.

The middle window at the back was relocated from the first church, its delicately patterned stained glass a contrast to the newer stained-glass windows outlining the nave. Despite the controversy surrounding the appliquéd reredos depicting the Virgin Mary and child Jesus – some thought its location behind the altar was inappropriate

and, in fact, it was once found in the refuse pile – it too remains one of the many illustrations of the members' continuing love of their spiritual home.

A reminder of their historical home is the lych-gate built by two parishioners in 1924. It is a close facsimile of a fifteenth-century structure in front of St. Leonard's Church in Heston, England, one of the few remaining lych-gates with a revolving gate operated by a stone weight and chain. The original purpose of a lych-gate was to protect the coffin as it rested at the entrance of the churchyard while the opening words of the burial service were read.

The lych-gate has never been used for that purpose at St. Mary the Virgin. If it's been used for its other tradition – as a kissing gate – nobody's telling. ⁊

The interior of St. Mary's Church, around 1915. The pointed arches so common to Anglican churches in the late nineteenth century are reflected in the apse windows, the communion rail, and the main arch leading into the apse. (Saskatchewan Archives Board R-B 3039)

Detail of the timber frame lych-gate, where tradition called for a funeral procession to stop for initial prayers before entering the church.

St. Andrew's Roman Catholic Church

NEAR WAPELLA

The excruciating excitement of Donald McKay and Archie MacDonald as they left their Scottish island homes for the wilds of western Canada is not difficult to imagine. It was spring 1883, and both were twenty and single. ❧ But what about Donald McDonald and his wife, Christy, sixty-six and sixty-four respectively? Or John and Christie McDonald, both thirty but with three children under the age of four, the youngest of whom, one-year-old Mary Margaret, died during the trip? Their thoughts are inconceivable. ❧ This mix of ages and circumstances, a total of "47 souls," left the Hebridean islands of Benbecula and South Uist on April 9 and arrived in Quebec May 3. At 1 a.m. on a frosty 24th of May,

St. Andrew's Church is similar to those designed by Oblate missionary-architect Brother Théodore de Byl, such as Sacred Heart Roman Catholic Church at Lebret. A rose window is featured directly below the bell.

a Canadian Pacific train deposited all but Mary Margaret at Wapella. Then, as Donald MacDiarmid wrote in his journal, "(We) came out to the Pipestone the next day with oxen and wagons with all our worldly possessions, to carve out homes on the prairie."

A year later, 240 more men, women, and children arrived from the same two islands. The oldest was seventy-five, and the youngest four months. As with the first group, all were crofters: families who had rented a small piece of land in Scotland. Their absentee landlord and sponsor of their move to Canada was Lady Gordon Cathcart of Aberdeenshire. Lady Cathcart, a Protestant, was known as a benefactor concerned about her crofters' welfare, but historians have noted that South Uist was one of the poorest Hebridean islands, and her tenants, mostly Roman Catholics, scrabbled to make a living on their arid plots. Although Lady Cathcart loaned about $500 for passage and supplies to each family who immigrated to the Pipestone area, she charged them five per cent interest, and modern scholars have concluded her motive was to increase profits by clearing her land of people.

Accustomed to hard work for little return, the Scots dug in – some even lived in dirt burrows at first – and eventually prospered. They were quick to declare their faith as well. In 1885, both the Presbyterians and the Roman Catholics built churches, the latter called St. Andrew's.

Oblate priests from St. Boniface were the first to preach at the log St. Andrew's, but they spoke English or French, and, as Donald MacDiarmid wrote, some of the listeners "had strong doubts as to whether the angels themselves could understand such unintelligible 'gibberish.'" When the Gaelic-speaking ecclesiastical student David Gillies of Nova Scotia arrived, therefore, he was embraced. And when he returned in 1888 as an ordained resident priest, his later plans to build a fieldstone church were similarly endorsed.

The site of the new edifice was an elevated clearing north of the Pipestone Valley, about ten kilometres south of Wapella and one kilometre from the original church. Records show each family agreed to provide a cord of fieldstone, but other details are sketchy. The Wapella local history, *Mingling Memories,* states that a St. Boniface architect and general contractor were hired, and names four parishioners who carried out much of the work. The booklet *A Short History of the Pioneer Scotch Settlers of St. Andrews, Sask.* lists one of the helpers, Alex McPherson, as a carpenter by trade and one, Donald McDougall, as a stonemason.

While the architect remains a mystery, his design recalls the traditional Roman Catholic churches of Quebec, albeit on a modest scale: the spire and rose window of the Gothic revival style combined with the round-arched windows of the Romanesque style.

The squared and coursed style of the stonemasonry is evidenced by the uniform shape and size of the stones, including those at the corners. Adding to the finished appearance are the Tyndall-stone windowsills and the careful sandstone arches, each composed of curved blocks resting on rectangular blocks and centred with a pink keystone.

Inside, each of the pews is divided into two boxes that were originally rented to parishioners and labelled with the family name. The barrel-vaulted ceiling above the two-storey apse is outlined with gold, and the two-storey ceiling above the centre aisle is coved and coffered with embossed, painted tin. At the centre of each of the thirty-three coffers, which represent the number of years Jesus lived on earth, is a symbolic painting by an unknown artist: a dagger, for example, refers to the piercing of Jesus's side during crucifixion.

The 1,640-pound (0.75 tonne) bronze bell, which is still rung for Sunday services from June to October, was allegedly the largest in the North-West Territories at the time. When Archbishop Langevin dedicated the church in October 1901, he blessed this bell in a separate ceremony that was too much for one Presbyterian girl who, in her letter to a friend, wrote, "We had stood for two hours and did not feel like standing another one."

Still, as this anonymous girl went on to write, the main ceremony and the church itself were worth every minute: "Words cannot tell to you what this church is like because it is so dazzling that you could spend days in it and still find some new beauty.

" . . . In conclusion, I will say it is almost too grand for words." ❧

A cemetery to the east of the church complements the quiet serenity of this rural religious complex.

Holy Trinity Anglican Church

NEAR PARADISE HILL

lthough located in an area visited by the earliest fur traders and missionaries – about ten kilometres west of the Carlton Trail – Holy Trinity Anglican Church at Deer Creek is one of the last churches in Saskatchewan to be built of fieldstone. Its architectural style, furthermore, refers to nineteenth-century Gothic revival in England, but its stonemasonry style is that of twentieth-century Germany. ❧ Holy Trinity's short history is due to the relatively recent arrival of settlers in the area along the North Saskatchewan River west of Paradise Hill. Alvin Moore and his wife, Millie, for example, homesteaded in 1910, among the first to farm at what eventually became known as Deer Creek. ❧ The Anglican Church was also slow to arrive. By the 1920s, however, a group of men were

The front of Deer Creek Church shows off the mortar treatment characteristic of the work of German stonemason Karl Gortzyk.

recruited in Great Britain to train as spiritual leaders at the Diocese of Saskatchewan's Bishop's College in Prince Albert. Locally known as "Bishop Lloyd's boys," they were ready to take on their priestly duties by the end of the decade, and one of them became the first incumbent at Fort Pitt Mission. He suggested building a church at Deer Creek.

This suggestion was received by willing hands with empty pocketbooks. But, with a grant from England, plans

were finally laid and volunteers stepped forward. In 1932, for example, the Methodist husband of an Anglican woman sent two of his hired men and a team of horses north about forty kilometres to Fiddler's Mill to cut logs and, after milling, haul home lumber for framing the church, which he also directed.

That same year, German stonemason Karl Gortzyk arrived in the district. His presence, together with the seemingly endless supply of

rocks in the area, prompted the idea of building a stone church. Accompanying Karl was John Le Grand, who had learned stonemasonry when he helped Karl build his parents' home. The two toured stone piles in the surrounding fields, split the stones they wanted, and left them for the farmers to haul to the building site.

Years later, the daughter of one of the church's eight founding families wrote of Karl: "He didn't want just any old stones; he wanted big rocks. It was most interesting to see him break a rock as big as a barrel with one or two good hard hits with a stone [maul] and the rock would split open."

Norman Moore was another child of a founding family. His father Alvin's pasture was across the road from the building site, and twelve-year-old Norman was enlisted to help with the construction. His horse, Major, was attached to a pulley that hoisted the stones up for placement in the tower. Norman also remembers Karl, "a short, stocky, comical guy," using forms to make the concrete blocks used for the quoins, tower crenellation, and the outline of the pointed-arch windows.

Norman's father was the rector's warden when, on Ascension Day in 1935, the Bishop of Saskatchewan consecrated the church. After the service, the 110 men, women and children in attendance walked across the road for a picnic lunch in Norman's father's pasture.

The furnishings for the church accumulated as slowly as the history. One local farmer fashioned the pulpit, and another built the pews, with each family buying its own and contributing extra to buy more. As with all rural churches in Saskatchewan, many furnishings were bought with funds raised by the Women's Auxiliary, and many were donated by relatives or friends of the church in England. The two leaded and stained glass windows behind the altar were donated in memory of a beloved mother.

The source of one donation, the church bell, was more unusual: Sir Henry Thornton was the second president of Canadian

National Railways and also the man responsible for CNR Radio, Canada's first coast-to-coast radio, forerunner of CBC. Sir Henry died in 1933, but Norman Moore assumes the bell was promised earlier, perhaps in 1928 when the crew laying the CNR tracks camped on his father's land.

Changes have occurred over the years – a metal roof has replaced the cedar shingles and, because the stone walls had been built directly on the prairie, a concrete slab was poured – but the stones have never been repointed. Nor do they show any need of such work.

Unlike so many other rural churches, furthermore, regular church services are held at Deer Creek. Norman Moore and his wife, Doris, are the only members, but the All Saints congregation from Fort Pitt joins them at Holy Trinity on alternate Sundays.

Norman is ensuring that worshipers will always find shelter in this broad, flat valley north of the North Saskatchewan. After the 2006 harvest was in, he organized a work bee to insulate Holy Trinity from the inside.

Deer Creek Church during construction. Note that the lower left portion of the mortar lacks its distinctive white final coat. (Norman Moore)

Standing outside in the bitter wind that sweeps down the valley, he double-checks the lock on the carved oak doors and says, "I want to get it done before I go. It's going to stand here a long time." ✻

After the consecration service in 1935, Bishop Bird *(centre)* joined Rev. Bolster and parishioners for an outdoor picnic. (Norman Moore)

OPPOSITE: Until the new gates and
brick gateposts were erected in recent
decades, Zion Evangelical Lutheran
Church at Wheatwyn stood alone on the
open prairie since its construction in 1907.
Inside, this small church features a balcony
that runs partly along the side wall,
above the north windows.

Zion Evangelical Lutheran Church

NEAR MARKINCH

Zion Evangelical Lutheran Church of Wheatwyn – as one of the founding fathers might have said, "*Armut ist keine schandeaber deswegen brauch mann nicht schmutzig und zerrissen herum laufen.*"* ❧ The descendants of those founding fathers are not poor, and, although church services were in German until the 1950s, some cannot even speak the language, but they still keep the church and its grounds, located thirteen kilometres southwest of Markinch, neat as a pin and scrupulously maintained. It's a trait passed on by the German-speaking men and women from what was then the Austro-Hungarian Empire, a collection of Eastern European countries that also included Bukovina. ❧ One of the first of these immigrants was Paul Blaser, who was fifteen when he left the homeland with his family in 1893.

The Canadian prairie is noted for its dramatic sunsets, one of which can be seen behind Wheatwyn Church

They settled at Neudorf, after which Paul worked on the Motherwell farm at Abernethy. He established his own homestead south of Markinch in 1899 and, five years later, held a meeting in his log-and-sod home with the intention of organizing a school district. The school, Wheatwyn, was built in 1905, with Paul as one of the first two trustees.

Paul was also one of the nine men remembered as organizers of Zion Evangelical Lutheran Church (later to incorporate the name Wheatwyn) in 1906. His brother Lorenz, as well as Kaspar Molder, Joseph Ulrich, Frederick Kaminski, Adam Markwart, Matthais Orb, Jacob Appenheimer and John Lingner were others.

Paul also figured prominently in the sticks and stones of the church. According to his third son, Lorenz, two Scottish stonemasons lived with Paul and his family while they built Wheatwyn Church and, immediately after, the fieldstone Blaser house, which was patterned on the Motherwell home.

The style of the squared, coursed and outlined stones of the Blaser home and the church are similar, while the shell of Bethlehem Lutheran Church, built about ten kilometres northwest of Wheatwyn around the same time by members of a different Lutheran synod, suggests a different stonemason. Although the pointed-arch windows of both churches are outlined in brick, Bethlehem's stones are laid in a random-rubble style, and its round-arched entrance and the round windows in each end gable suggest a mason with more flare.

As indicated by the huge limestone cornerstone, Wheatwyn Church was dedicated in 1907. The interior was largely unfurnished at that time, as the Sherlock-Manning pump organ didn't arrive until 1912, and the pulpit, altar, and baptismal font were made by Leopold Schneider, who arrived to homestead in the district in 1913. A gallery over the entrance and along one side was probably added later to accommodate the new and expanding families of the congregation.

This gallery provided plenty of illicit fun for young boys who, when their parents were outside, would scamper up its steep stairs and return to the main floor via the deep window wells. The warmest childhood memories of the church, in fact, are more sec-ular than religious. One woman, for example, recalled wearing and admiring her new Eaton's catalogue dress at one of the annual Christmas Eve services and being dis-tracted from her self-regard by a fire caused by the live candles in the tree. And all remember the potluck supper, skits, and songs of the year's highlight, *Famelien Abend*.[†]

More-sobering stories lie in the adjacent cemetery. The earliest stone has two dates: one for Johann Lingner, who died in 1902 at nineteen, and one for his brother Georg, who died in 1904 at the same age. They were buried on Lingner property and, when land was needed for the church and cemetery, the boys' father, another of

the nine church founders, donated the land around them.

Today, in addition to the Lingner headstone and many others, there are a number of black iron crosses. They mark known graves that had no stone or name. These crosses speak as eloquently of the respect for those who have gone before as the plaque noting the 1982 designation of the church as a municipal heritage site.

Although dwindling mem-bership and the inconvenience of heating the church with one potbelly stove resulted in closure of the church in 1961, annual memorial services con-tinue to celebrate the faith that sustained the pioneering congregation. And this faith is never more clearly portrayed

Karl Hinrichs, who lived in Saskatchewan for several years before returning to the Netherlands, photographed Wheatwyn Church in 1968. The squared mortar joints are clearly visible in his image. (Saskatchewan Archives Board R-B 4139(1)

than in a small plaque on one wall: simple but, because of the Gothic-style, Old German script, the most decorative item in the church, it states, "*E R kann helfen.*"[‡]

---

[*] There is an excuse for being poor but no excuse for being dirty and tattered.

[†] Family evening.

[‡] God can help.

The interior of the church reveals an unusual feature: a balcony built over the seating along the north wall.

St. Andrew's Anglican Church

HEWARD

S t. Andrew's Church at Heward is a gem set in what is now the snaggle-toothed village of Heward. Literally and metaphorically, it rises above graying buildings and a caragana gone wild to amaze the occasional highway traveller drawn in by its broach spire and crooked cross. ❧ The word *medieval* comes to the mind of such visitors, and they are not wrong. Dr. Malcolm Thurlby, professor of visual arts at Toronto's York University, writes: "The 1921 Anglican church at Heward may be loosely described as Early English," a term that, he states, has been used to categorize the first phase of English Gothic. "I say 'loosely' because none of the features suggest a first-hand reference to English 13th-century sources, either through the direct knowledge of the architect or via books/manuals on English Gothic

The variety of stones used to build
St. Andrew's Church gives the massing
a rich colour, and helps bring out the
detail of the buttress construction.
Stone churches rarely include
a full basement.

architecture. The simple pointed windows, nave buttresses and steeply pointed roof all follow Gothic principles, however, and there are also precedents for tower-porches in 12th- and 13th-century churches in England."

This assessment is borne out by St. Andrew's history. The first homesteaders in the district arrived in 1900, followed several years later by the Canadian Pacific Railroad. A frame St. Andrew's Church officially opened in 1905 and served a wide and increasingly populated district until Rev. Frederick Pike arrived in 1917.

Rev. Pike was born in Gorton, Manchester, England, and, after training as a priest in Manitoba and Saskatchewan, was ordained by the Diocese of Qu'Appelle in Regina. In a 1921 diocesan publication, he wrote of the excavation for the church the same year he arrived, the four hundred loads of prairie stone hauled by farmers "as a labour of love," and two hundred loads of sand from Rock Lake thirteen kilometres away. By 1918, his account continued, the foundation was built of stone to ground level but, "During the past four years there has been a crop failure each year, which has made it increasingly difficult to complete the church . . . Will anyone help in this important work to provide a House of God for the children of the prairie?"

That help must have arrived, for on October 18, 1921, the stone St. Andrew's Church was officially opened.

A variety of documents reveal further details. While local lore has the church being a copy of an English one that had been lost to the sea due to erosion, a 1961 letter from Canon Pike in Victoria, British Columbia, states that St. Andrews is a copy of a thirteenth-century church near Oxford, England. A July 1919 edition of the *Manitoba Free Press* states that A. J. Rowley of Regina was the architect.

A parishioners' church history tells of the builder and contractor being W. R. Brown and Company of Weyburn, the carpentry by L. Satrums of Creelman, the millwork by Regina Door and Sash Company, and the nine memorial windows by McCaw, Stevenson and Company of Belfast, Ireland. A local blacksmith made the cross from metal sleigh runners and, to the embarrassment of parishioners, it assumed its drunken slant soon after it was attached.

Not surprisingly, given the relatively messy masonry work, no stonemason is mentioned.

No explanation is given for the cornerstone either: it was laid in 1919 by the grand master and the deputy grand master of the Saskatchewan Grand Lodge of Free Masons. The stone bears the freemason square-and-compass insignia. According to provincial freemason records, Rev. Pike was a Mason, and during the period of time that St. Andrews was built, it was not uncommon for

that organization to be asked to lay cornerstones because of its self-proclaimed link to ancient stonemasons.

While the interior included the open timbered ceiling and the raised chancel of traditional medieval design, some of the furnishings were the real thing. Rev. Pike's 1961 letter, in which he refers to the small north projection as a "chapel," tells the story of these items. While on a fund-raising trip to England, he was offered a thirteenth-century stone font that originally came from a Cornwall church partially submerged in water at high tide; an oak lectern from a Powick, Worcestershire, church where the pews were hand-carved in the fifteenth century; and a chapel altar from the (demolished) private chapel of Sir Robert Peel.

According to Canon Pike's letter, the small chapel altar was given to the Kisbey Anglican Church in 1961, the year St. Andrew's was bought by the United Church. The fate of the thirteenth-century font and other artifacts is unknown. Even worse is the fate of the building: although

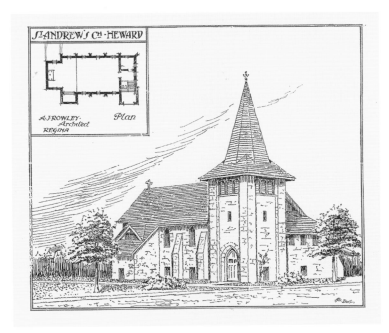

designated a municipal heritage property in 1983, it has not been used since it closed in 1968.

It remains in remarkably good condition, however, perhaps because of unseen forces: a painting of the church in a Heward home shows an angel grasping the tilted cross. Who could argue? ❧

Few architectural drawings of Saskatchewan's stone churches have survived. This presentation drawing demonstrates the fine artistic talents of architects in the time before computer generation. (Diocese of Qu'Appelle Archives: R-705, file VII. 89)

Public Buildings

Public buildings are so often cold in appearance, but not the stone Watrous Pumphouse and the chalets overlooking Kenosee and Little Manitou Lakes. Not even in winter. Perhaps it's the ageless beauty of the stones, each native to the surrounding fields and hillsides and thus part of the land. Perhaps it's the hands that chose the stone, examining each for colour, size, shape and heft, then placing it just so. This care, this precision, this soul still speaks.

ieldstone was not commonly used for public buildings in western Canada, the preferred material being wood or brick for smaller communities, and brick or finely cut Tyndall stone for the larger urban centres. ❧ One of the more interesting fieldstone municipal buildings was the Whitewood Town Hall, which included a two-storey front section and a community hall behind. This structure featured brick quoins at the corners and around the window and door surrounds. Although it was reportedly designed by Alexander Fraser of Indian Head, the similarities with the workmanship of Wapella stonemason Richard Talmay suggest another option. The town hall stood until 1983, when it was demolished to make way for a new municipal building. ❧ A few municipal utilities buildings were also made of stone,

This chalet (right) and dining hall, part of a government make-work project during the early years of the Great Depression, were the heart and Rustic soul of Saskatchewan's first provincial park, located at Little Manitou Lake.

The chalet at Kenosee Lake, Moose Mountain Provincial Park, with extensive stone-bordered landscaping. (Saskatchewan Archives Board R-A 10,985–2)

again reflecting the need for a strong, long-lasting facility even though they served a very utilitarian purpose. Structures such as power plants, streetcar garages, and

pumphouses were artfully designed to make them blend more aesthetically within the community. One of the most impressive such structures is the diminutive Watrous Pumphouse, located at the east end of Manitou Lake. Many similar structures, like the pumphouses at Kerrobert and Tilney, were made of brick, and constructed in co-operation with the local railway company to provide water for both the municipality and the boilers for steam locomotives.

Governments were more likely to use fieldstone in the construction of municipal structures such as bridges and dams, where they were often used to build piers and other foundation requirements. While bridges built entirely of fieldstone are a fairly common sight in eastern Canada, very few such structures were built in the West. One of those was at the Saskatchewan Hospital in North Battleford. Like many older wooden and steel bridges, most stone bridges have been replaced with modern structures more capable of handling larger and heavier traffic.

The stone pumphouse for the Town of Watrous was situated at the east end of Little Manitou Lake, about thirteen kilometres away from the community. (Library and Archives Canada PA 38544)

By far the largest number of fieldstone public buildings were erected in the provincial and national parks in the 1920s and 1930s, as part of a continental move to establish rustic yet comfortable park facilities. The chalets at Moose Mountain and Little Manitou Lake provincial parks, along with some of their associated tourist cabins, all reflected this trend in the developing tourism industry. 🎋

The town hall in Whitewood included a projecting balcony above the centre entry, and a tin parapet with four pinnacles and a triangular pediment. It was demolished in 1983. (Saskatchewan Archives Board R-B 12,485)

OPPOSITE: The dining hall featured a large A-frame gable over the primary entrance.

Little Manitou Chalet & Dining Hall

MANITOU BEACH

The prospectus for the Manitou Lake Sanitarium & Mineral Products Manufacturing Co. and the date of the letter responding to it set the scene. ❧ The prospectus included plans for an eighteen-hole golf course, a "magnificent hotel," and a plant that would use extractions from Little Manitou Lake to manufacture oils to cure piles, colds, eczema, rheumatism and dandruff, as well as tablets guaranteed to cure constipation. ❧ Saskatchewan Premier James Gardiner's response to this prospectus stated his complete confidence in the success of the venture. His letter was dated March 12, 1929. ❧ Seven months later, the North American stock market crashed, and Saskatchewan was one of the first casualties. Within a year, the federal and provincial governments were sharing the cost of relief work-camps,

One of the two primary buildings at Camp Easter Seal, originally used as the chalet for Little Manitou Provincial Park. Cobblestones were the usual exterior building material for natural parks throughout much of North America in the 1930s.

one of which was at Little Manitou Lake on part of the land intended for the Manitou Lake Sanitarium.

The concept of building what a 1930/31 government report called "a watering place and tourist camp" was similar to that of the "magnificent hotel": to accommodate well-heeled visitors drawn by the health benefits of a lake that was compared to Germany's famous Carlsbad Springs.

These benefits were first recognized by First Nations people – *Manitow* is Cree for "Great Spirit" – who brought their sick to the lake to be cured by the high content of salt and other minerals caused by evaporation of snowmelt, rainfall, and spring water in a land depression without inlet or outlet. By 1910, local entrepreneurs were building bathhouses, and by the 1920s, Manitou Beach was one of the leading resorts in western Canada.

While aiming to make money from those who would partake of these waters, the government's main goal for the construction of a chalet was to employ as many workmen as possible. And this was best done with buildings of the labour-intensive Rustic style.

The Rustic style dates to the mid-1870s, when the Adirondack style was developed to lure wealthy vacationers to upstate New York. Adopting some Swiss chalet features, it was intended to harmonize with the environment and make use of local material such as timber and fieldstone. By the early twentieth century, the Rustic style had become synonymous with North American national parks.

Because of the glacial meltwater that once roared through the Watrous Spillway, of which Little Manitou Lake is a remnant, stones and boulders litter the fields above the lake and were therefore a practical choice for the creation of rusticity. Their collection by local farmers, furthermore, provided extra employment: one man's childhood memory, for example, is of loading stones into the family's "Bennett buggy" – a car pulled by horses, and named after Canada's prime minister at the time – to haul to the building site.

The use of uncut fieldstones can limit style, however, so they were applied as a veneer. The original roof of the chalet was thatched, but weather and rodents soon caused its replacement with cedar shingles. Still, the typical picturesque appearance of the Rustic style remained intact, and was carried through to the interior with its stone fireplace and pillars and the geometric wall patterns created with twigs. Like the original gables of the chalet, the cabins around the chalet featured Tudor-style half-timbering made from logs, another Rustic characteristic.

According to vitriolic letters to the editor in the May 1931 *Watrous Signal,* these features were not necessarily part of the original design. John Pinder-Ross, who is listed in the 1929 Henderson's Directory as an architect with the Regina firm W. C. Van Egmond and Stan Storey, wrote, "The chalet and other buildings designed by me were 15–16th century English architecture, the conception being a manor house with the park as a surrounding estate laid out in relation to the main building with the retainer-peasant cottages placed in scenic positions." Pinder-Ross claimed his design was altered by the construction committee.

While no official records of the final designer remain, it is recorded that 450 men, each

earning $20 a month, were employed in the construction of the chalet, its associated cabins, and other buildings in 1930/31. During the following fiscal year, a nine-hole golf course, the Rustic-style dining hall, and various amenities were added.

Little Manitou Provincial Park was officially opened in June 1931. It was the first of the six provincial parks to open that year, all of them the result of the Depression and also the province's new control over natural resources. Until the late 1940s, it was the most popular of all the provincial parks.

In 1945, however, a commission was appointed to study the park facilities and the medicinal properties of Little Manitou Lake. Owners of the clinics and baths were also interviewed about their some-

times extravagant claims for cures. The commission's 1946 report, which included fears about the declining level of the lake and the statement, "In most cases treatment is completely unscientific and some cases might be dangerous," may be one reason why, ten years later, the chalet and surrounding buildings were leased to the Saskatchewan Council for Crippled Children and Adults, now the Saskatchewan Abilities Council, for one dollar a year.

Located outside what became a regional park in 1961, the Manitou complex is now known as Camp Easter Seal. For three months every year, its combination of form and function enhances and often changes forever the lives of both campers and staff, a rare achievement for any site. ❧

The two main buildings at Little Manitou Lake were initially roofed with thatched straw. However, this proved impractical, and the roofs were soon redone with cedar shingles. (Saskatchewan Archives Board R-B 8667)

Watrous Pumphouse

MANITOU BEACH

The "aerator" at the east end of Little Manitou Lake near Watrous seemed like a good idea at the time. ❧ Odiferous water – "It was stinky, stinky. Smelled like rotten egg," says Lillian Sellers, whose father was the Watrous waterworks engineer – was pumped to a circular concrete cistern punctured with many openings near the top. Resting on the cistern was a round frame structure with a conical roof and a cupola, where pipes and nozzles squirted water in all directions to "aerate" and thus freshen it. Not surprisingly, the aerator was a failure. ❧ The fieldstone pumphouse beside the aerator, on the other hand, did exactly what it was supposed to do for its entire functional life, and it remains one of the finest examples of skilled stonework in the province. ❧ Considering the utilitarian purpose, the design and

The sheet-metal roof is another prominent feature of the pumphouse, and one that has withstood decades of weathering without replacement. Buildings with this fine architectural design are more commonly found in urban settings than in an isolated rural environment.

the stonework are particularly impressive. The symmetry of the building, as well as the graceful lines of its doors and windows, are classically pleasing, while the masonry attests to the artistic eye that guided it: cobblestone walls highlight the cut-fieldstone arches and quoins; a string course of rectangular cut stone marks the level at which the foundation flares outward; and each of the shaped stones is outlined with a raised joint, a decorative and difficult technique

that bespeaks the mason's care and pride in his work.

The beauty of the pumphouse, furthermore, is more than cosmetic. The walls have never needed repointing and the faux-tile metal roof is original

This artistry and craftsmanship cannot be attributed to anyone – neither the designer nor the stonemason is recorded – but some of its history can be pieced together. The Grand Trunk Pacific Railway established Watrous

as a divisional point on the line in 1908, and an adequate water supply for both the town and the railway's steam engines was a problem almost immediately. By 1912, states *Prairie Reflections: A History of Watrous,* the railway contributed to the financing of a well at the east end of Little Manitou Lake.

The earliest extant record of the pumphouse is a copy of a 1914 plan of the Watrous "waterworks," which shows a pipeline from a pumphouse on today's site to a water tower on the west side of Watrous, about thirteen kilometres as the crow flies, which is how the line was laid. This drawing is stamped with "Chipman and Power" of "Toronto and Winnipeg," one of Canada's earliest consulting engineering firms in the field of water and waste water. A 1915 plan on linen, similar to the 1914 plan but with an enlarged drawing of the pumphouse, is attributed to the Grand Trunk Pacific with additional notes by Chipman and Power.

Lillian Sellers's father became the waterworks engineer in 1922 and, along with his wife and two young boys, lived in the pumphouse until a small house was built beside it about two years later. Their living quarters in the pumphouse then became the office, which Lillian, who was born in 1926, remembers as occupying about one-quarter of the main floor. She says the remaining space was taken by a malodorous kerosene pump on a concrete slab extending up from the basement.

Located in a hollow, the land around the pumphouse was studded with soft-water wells with manhole covers, but there still wasn't enough water to meet the demand. In the early 1930s, therefore, a well was drilled at a freshwater lake about two kilometres south of the pumphouse. This was the source of the highly sulphurated water, as well as the reason for the construction of the aerator and the arrival of electricity to operate the new pump.

In 1939, reports Lillian, a well was drilled about two kilometres northwest of the pumphouse, with a pipe laid under the end of the lake. This "north well" finally resolved the problem of insufficient potable water.

After being decommissioned in the mid-1960s, the pumphouse lay empty until 1995, when it was bought by nineteen-year-old Aaron Farago of Manitou Beach. Aaron, who had played around the pumphouse as a child, thought its renovation would be an extension of his restoration work on cars and furniture. He discovered otherwise. First he had to build a road into the property, then clear the land of pipes and brush, and clean out old trenches to restore drainage into the nearby creek instead of the basement. Finally, he replaced the two-metre-high windows,

re-faced the "shot gunned" front door, and rebuilt the main floor to create an open space enclosed by the original red-brick-lined walls and six-metre-high, tongue-and-groove fir ceiling.

All this and much more led him to sell it to another young man in 2001. Both realized the magnitude of the renovation project only after they took it on, but neither has regrets. Because of its designation as a municipal heritage property, its renewed beauty and dignity will continue to surprise and delight others as much as it has them. ❧

A man, possibly the resident engineer, walks along the causeway leading away from the pumphouse, carrying a pail – perhaps for picking the many saskatoon berries in the area. (Saskatchewan Archives Board: R-A 7814)

Moose Mountain Chalet

NEAR KENOSEE LAKE

Any account of Saskatchewan during the 1930s, when the Great Depression was exacerbated by a killing drought, is one of almost unrelieved misery. Almost. One of the attempts to relieve this misery was the creation of make-work projects, such as building fieldstone chalets on the shores of both Little Manitou and Kenosee lakes. Unlike many ideas conceived during desperate times, however, these two projects remain treasures of Saskatchewan's architectural past. Still, while both chalets were the result of the government's attempt at conservation and social assistance, they differed right from the beginning. ❧ Their joint origin was due to the transfer of natural resources from the federal government to the provinces in 1930 and, later that year, the federal government's agreement to

Although most of the original cottages were demolished in the 1990s, a few have been preserved to illustrate the type of accommodations provided to the public throughout much of the twentieth century.

share the cost of dealing with the unemployment caused by the Depression. Relief camps were immediately established across the province, with the largest at Little Manitou Lake, where 450 men earned $1 a day building the chalet, and a much smaller one at the Moose Mountain Forest Reserve Park, where 55 men received 77 cents a day to carry out park improvements only.

The Moose Mountain Forest Reserve Park had been created in 1896. It was composed of 154 acres of ash, aspen and white birch on an elevation of land created fifty million years

ago and pockmarked with hundreds of water-filled depressions that appeared after the Wisconsin glacier retreated. The biggest of the depressions was Fish Lake, where nearby homesteaders and Cannington Manor gentility built cabins and a resort in the 1890s.

By December 1931, seven provincial parks had been created, one of which was the former Moose Mountain Forest Reserve. Two relief camps subsequently operated at Moose Mountain, and according to the Department of Natural Resources 1931/32 annual report, one "was

employed in the construction of a large stone chalet and 14 cabins . . . a sunken garden . . . and clearing of a fireguard that may be utilized as a golf course."

According to the daughter of C. F. Christopher, a 1903 Fish Lake hotel owner, the chalet was sited where wild ferns grew. It was designed by provincial architect Harold Dawson, and built by stone-mason Charlie Parker of nearby Kennedy. Dawson's plans show what today would be called a two-storey walkout. Built into a gentle slope to the lake, its lower level contained the main entrance, a Tudor-arched door that led into a central "rotunda" surrounded by offices, utility rooms and the manager's suite. A staircase on one side led up to a central dining room with a vaulted, two-storey ceiling. On each side of this open ceiling were four guest bedrooms.

The chalet's Rustic style was not as pure as that at Little Manitou. The concrete walls were veneered with fieldstone but, although the architectural plans show a cobblestone surface, Charlie Parker created a much more formal appearance with cut field-stone, each with a raised joint. Other Rustic features that survived the drawing board were "hand-sawn and re-split" cedar shakes on the roof, and "round timbers" in the back, front, and side gables. The latter, the half-timbering of gables, illustrated the Tudor influence on the Rustic style. The cabins around the chalet were partially clad with cobblestone and half-timbering.

Inside, the dining room was rusticated with a large fieldstone fireplace and log ceiling beams. The floor was of "clear birch," which may have come from the surrounding forest.

Premier James Anderson officially opened the chalet in July 1932, using the new name for Fish Lake, Kenosee, a word translated from the Cree word for fish, *kinosew,* another emphasis on the wilderness theme.

The premier's address included the statement, "The policy of the government is to establish Provincial Parks throughout the province as playgrounds for the people." But, by that time, the development and expansion of parks was included in the government's reduction of expenditures due to the ongoing Depression.

In November 1933, however, a fire destroyed everything but the chalet's exterior walls. It was officially called an accident, but there were those who swore it was set and said they knew who did it. Reconstruction began the following spring. The chalet and cabins, after all, were the major source of revenue, and Moose Mountain Park was second only to Little Manitou in popularity.

Some changes were carried out during reconstruction. The fieldstone fireplace was rebuilt with brick, and the timbers on the gables and the new, flat dining-room ceiling became milled beams.

Changes continued in subsequent years. The dining room moved to the lower level, and more rooms were added to the second level in the mid-1960s. That level became administrative offices in the 1970s, and the lower level became a tea room. Today, the lower level is a visitors' interpretive centre.

The circular drive and peony-lined path to the shore are now gone, but the sunken garden is still brilliant with flowers. Evergreens tower over the expansive lawn, framing a view of the low, forested hills outlining Kenosee Lake. And on weekends, it all comes alive: wedding parties and their photographers; artists selling work from their studios in the surrounding cabins; and tourists who can still detect the bygone elegance of silver and linen and dressing for dinner.

The chalet, in short, remains the gemstone in a park that is still one of the most popular "playgrounds for the people." ❧

Very few changes have been made to the chalet since this photo was taken in 1948. Trees have matured, and parking has been moved from the south to the north side of the building. (Saskatchewan Archives Board R-A 10,985–2)

Ruins

Ruins: the mystery, the mystery, the mystery! Who among us can resist a ruin?

*M*any old stone structures around the province are falling down. Despite this, they are still very attractive, not so much for their original design but how they now appear as ruins on the landscape. ❧ Indeed, in many parts of the world, ruins are among the most visited historic attractions. The Coliseum in Rome is a prime example. Yet, in North America, there appears to be an aversion to preserving such features. More often than not, stone buildings that no longer have a viable economic function for the property owner have been demolished. ❧ To conclude this book, we present for your enjoyment images of some of the ruins that we have encountered during the past few years. We hope you will find them as impressive as we did, and that you will think twice if you should ever contemplate removing an old historic landmark from the Saskatchewan landscape. ❧

TOP LEFT: Bethlehem Lutheran Church, southwest of Markinch, was deliberately burned to prevent desecration and vandalism of the abandoned building.

TOP RIGHT: An old gambrel-roofed barn gradually collapses near Lumsden.

BOTTOM: A farm near Gainsborough.

TOP : In 2001, the crumbling ruin of a stone church framed the Lipton grain elevator in the distance.

BOTTOM LEFT: A once stately farmhouse crumbles under its own weight near Oxbow.

BOTTOM RIGHT: Remnants of a once substantial farmhouse near Avonhurst.

TOP LEFT: The roof appears to have been ripped off this well-designed and well-built farmhouse near Grenfell.

TOP RIGHT: This barn foundation at Buffalo Pound Lake has been stabilized to prevent further deterioration.

BOTTOM: Remnants of a house foundation in the Southey area.

ACKNOWLEDGEMENTS

This book could not have been produced without the co-operation of the Saskatchewan Heritage Foundation in providing unrestricted access to material from Cec and Susan Hayward's Heritage Grant Project. A condition of receiving a grant from the Foundation is that the resultant material be made available to other researchers. Therefore, just as the Haywards have shared their stone buildings research data with us, we hope that others will build on the information that we have amassed in the production of this book. Neither study is definitive, and we look forward to seeing future publications dealing with the rich heritage that can be found in Saskatchewan's stone buildings. ❧ We particularly wish to recognize the contributions of Terri Lefebvre Prince and Dr. Bill Brennan, who provided valuable historical information and, due to their fastidious examination of a draft manuscript, identified errors and inconsistencies.

PHOTOGRAPHY:

Many photos were also taken by Dorothy Easton, as she accompanied and helped Larry on his journeys through the province. Examples of her work can be found on the following pages: 17, 36(right), 37, 38, 62, 72, 73, 80, 107, 108, 111, 112 (right), 113, 126, 135, 151, 175, 183, 214, 227, 235, 236, 237, 241 (centre left), 241 (bottom right), 242 (bottom left), 243 (top left), 246 (bottom right), and 247 (bottom left). Authors photographs: Marg Hryniuk by Barry Lane; Frank Korvemaker by Cory Rainville; and Larry Easton by Dorothy Easton.

INDIVIDUALS:

The production of this book also involved the assistance of many people and organizations. Some have contributed historical or anecdotal information and historic photographs. Others have given of their time to guide us to the stone buildings on or near their property, or have provided essential directions on how to find those buildings, that "you can't miss". We have tried to keep diligent records of all those who helped us in any manner, and apologize for any whose names might have been inadvertently omitted.

Among those who were so helpful to us are the following people: Brian Acton, Morgan Adam, Lavada Arnold, Bob Arscott, Maurice Arsenault, Lloyd Arthur, Gino Astolfi, Charlie Baer, Bryce Bailey, Foster Barnsley, Deanna Bates, George Beatty, Garry Bernard, Verna Betker, Dorothy Bjarnson, Lawrence Blaser, Paul Blaser, Cindy Blondeau, Anna Blythman, Ethel Box, Dr. Bill Brennan, Bernard and Elizabeth Brown, Harry Burke, Don Bushe, Bob Campbell, Trent Catley, Beatrice Chabot, Cliff Chatterson, Greg Chatterson, Annie Chervinski, Darrell Clark, Helen Clark, Jackie Clark, Mrs. Adam Colquhoun, Bill Crampton, Venetia Crawford, Norma Crossman, Della Crosson, Will and Sue Crosson, Arnold Dale, Dr. Janis Dale, Ken Dalgarno, Denise Dash, Barry Dearle, Earl and Margaret Debenham, Mr. Dickie, Audrey Doidge, Shaun Douglas, Duane Dreger, Michael and Kathryn Drope, Albert Dubé, Andre Dubois, Nathan Dufour, David Dunn, Barry Elmer, Genevieve Etcheverry, Marie and Dennis Everett, Aaron Farago, Debbie Farago, Bruce Farrer, Trish Fink, Mildred Finny, Bernie Flaman, Jim Focht, Gary Fortin, Ivy Galbraith, Alvin and Eva Gallinger, Destiny Gibney, Kathleen Gieni, Eugene Gonczy, Grant Gordon, Ewald Gossner, Roy Grier, John Griffin, Doretta Halek, Margaret Hall, Marty Halpape, Janette Hamilton, Andree Harkness, Doreen Harman, Jean Harris, Derek Harrison, Corrie Hart, Ron Hart, Donna Harvey, Jim Henry, Phyllis Henry, Ross Herrington, Trevor Herriot, Peter Ho, Jackie Hobbs, Russ & Pam Hodgins, Vangie Hogart, Dr. and Mrs. Stuart Houston, Randy and Barb Irvin, Pearl Jamison, Jim Jeeves, Rose Kacsmar, Lorna Keene, Orvin Kent, Wayne Kent, Jim King, Rob Kinley, Mrs. E. Kitchen, Shelia Korchinski, Jason Kovacs, Rick Krehbiel, Benedikt Kuhn, Gary Lang, Mildred Lang, Gary Langrish, Jim LaRocque, Pauline Larre, Albert Laval, Giles Lesage, Doreen Lloyd, Darcy Lockerman, Glen Lorenze, Kilby MacBean, Don MacFarlane, John Madison, Marie Mahan, Leslie Maitland, Albert Ma, Kilby MacBean, Don MacFarlane, Marie Mahan, Dave Martin, Cindy Maurer, Albert May,

Evelyn McAdam, Bill McCall, Dave McCall, Don McGowan, Laurie McLaren, Robert McLaren, David McLennan, Peter McMullen, Grace McNally, Marian McRobbie, Dean James Merritt, Flo Miller, Iona Miller, Jack Mollard, Norman and Doris Moore, Carla Motz, Kasper Moulder, Joyce Muir, Derek Muldoon, W.K. Mysyk, Ann Nargan, Darcy Neestom, Sharon Nelson, Pat Nichols, Helen Norman, Tim Novak, Sherry Noyes, Doreen Oakes, Suzanne Pambrun, Kay Parley, Richard Partridge, David & Debbie Pearson, Mary Ann Pearson, Donna Petterson, Bill Pook, Betty Popowich, Sheila Potts, Trevor Powell, Ron and Monica Price, Terri Lefebvre Prince, Garth Pugh, Jack Ramm, Brian & Sandra Reeve, Doug Remkie, Anita Ring, Kathy and Ron Robb, Leigh Robinson, Brenda Rodgers, Ken and Dave Rosin, Al Rosseker, Lois and Bob Rowe, Jim Rubin, Lyn Russell, Bo Ruzicka, Dorothy Schaffel, Anna Schaffer, Denise Schmitz, Herb Schneider, Emil Sebulski, Lillian Sellers, Wayne Sexsmith, Jim Shaw, Leigh Shaw, Richard Shaw, Peter Shenher, Nora Singleton, Joyce Smith, Larry Snodgrass, Francis Sokalski, Helen Solmes, Dave Sorenson, Donald Sorenson, Jean Sproule, Betty & Larry Stanley, Bob and Laura Stanley, Lee and Laura Stanley, Roy Stanley, Annette and Ward Stebner, Elizabeth Stevenson, David Stewart,

Donald Henry Sutherland, Mrs. Albert Syrota, Lois Tanner, Dion Tarasoff, James Taylor, Phyllis Taylor, Ed & Harold Tetzlaff, Abe Thompson, Dr. Malcolm Thurlby, Bill Tingley, Elizabeth Tomalak, Marjorie Toth, Karen Totten, Cindy Tulloch, Shirley Van Kennell, Joan Velestuk, Ken Verhaeghe, Phyllis Verhaeghe, June Wagman, Gilbert Wagner, Dr. Bill Waiser, Faith Ward, Bob Watson, David Watson, Trina and Scott Watson, Doreen Westcott, Donny White, Yvonne Wildman, Darryl Wiles, Alex Wiley, Victoria Williams, Ron Wolfe, Barry Woolhouse, Gary Wyatt, Melanie Yanoshewski, Werner Zerbin, Roy Zinkhan.

ORGANIZATIONS:

We have also benefited from the co-operation and assistance provided by various staff in heritage organizations, public libraries, archives and other agencies, including: Archdiocese of Regina; Archives Deschatelets, Ottawa, Ontario; Broadview Museum; Broadview Town Office; CBC Radio; City of Yorkton Archives; Diefenbaker Canada Centre, University of Saskatchewan; Diocese of Qu'Appelle Archives, Regina; Diocese of Saskatchewan Archives, Prince Albert; Esplanade Heritage & Heritage Centre, Medicine Hat, Alberta; Grenfell Museum; Hastings Museum and Art Gallery, Hastings, England; Indian Head Museum; Information Services Corporation; Library and Archives Canada; Moose Jaw Public Library, Archives; Moosomin Town Office; Parks Canada; Pontiac Archives, Quebec; Regina Public Library, Local History Room; Saskatchewan Abilities Council; Saskatchewan Architectural Heritage Society; Saskatchewan Archives Board; Saskatchewan Tourism, Parks, Culture and Sport Culture, Youth and Recreation, Heritage Branch; Saskatchewan Environment; Saskatchewan Genealogical Society; Saskatchewan Heritage Foundation; Saskatchewan Hospital, North Battleford; Saskatchewan Research Council; Saskatoon Public Library, Local History Room; University of Regina, Library; University of Saskatchewan, Archives; Watrous Town Office.

FINANCIAL ASSISTANCE:

The authors gratefully acknowledge the financial assistance received from the Saskatchewan Heritage Foundation, in co-operation with Saskatchewan Lotteries, and SaskCulture Inc

FAMILY:

We each had generous support from our respective families during the past several years. This came not only through words of encouragement, but also through giving up time together so that work on the book could be undertaken.

PUBLISHER'S ACKNOWLEDGEMENTS

Coteau Books would like to acknowledge the financial support of the Saskatchewan Architectural Heritage Society in the publication of this book.

ABOUT THE AUTHORS

This book brings together the various talents of three Saskatchewanians:

MARGARET HRYNIUK'**s** newspaper and magazine articles have included heritage buildings ever since she won a 1979 Saskatchewan Writers' Guild award for her story on the 1897 brick-and-fieldstone Hudson's Bay Company store at Fort Qu'Appelle. She is also the author of *A Tower of Attraction: An Illustrated History of Government House, Regina, Saskatchewan* and co-author of *Regina: A City of Beautiful Homes.*

LARRY EASTON is a Regina-based freelance photographer and regularly contributes images to *Prairies North* magazine. He has a knack for bringing out the character and warmth of historic construction. His images portray the natural beauty of stone and help demonstrate why stonemasons would select certain stones for their work. In addition, his keen eye often finds some associated natural or peripheral feature that makes his photographs so appealing.

FRANK KORVEMAKER is a construction historian who has been involved with the documentation, preservation, and development of many of Saskatchewan's heritage sites for over a quarter of a century. In this book, he focuses his attention on providing general overviews of the various chapters, and on some of the stonemasons without whom none of these buildings could have been possible. He was the principal photographer for *Historic Architecture of Saskatchewan,* published by the Saskatchewan Association of Architects.